I0120075

Secret Exploits

Of Admiral Richard E. Byrd
The Hollow Earth, Nazi Occultism,
Secret Societies And The JFK Assassination

TIMOTHY G. BECKLEY, PUBLISHER

Secret Exploits
Of Admiral Richard E. Byrd
The Hollow Earth, Nazi Occultism,
Secret Societies And The JFK Assassination

Contributors:
Timothy Green Beckley, Tim Cridland, Sean Casteel, Tim R. Swartz, Micah Hanks,
Dianne Robbins, Richard Toronto, Dr. Raymond Bernard

Copyright 2017 by Timothy Green Beckley
dba Global Communications/Conspiracy Journal

All rights reserved. No part of these manuscripts may be copied or reproduced by any mechanical or digital methods and no exerpts or quotes may be used in any other book or manuscript without permission in writing by the Publisher, Global Communications/ Conspiracy Journal, except by a reviewer who may quote brief passages in a review.

Published in the United States of America By
Global Communications/Conspiracy Journal
Box 753 · New Brunswick, NJ 08903

Staff Members
Timothy G. Beckley, Publisher
Carol Ann Rodriguez, Assistant to the Publisher
Sean Casteel, General Associate Editor
Tim R. Swartz, Graphics and Editorial Consultant
William Kern, Editorial and Art Consultant

Sign Up On The Web For Our Free Weekly Newsletter
and Mail Order Version of Conspiracy Journal
and Bizarre Bazaar
www.ConspiracyJournal.com

Order Hot Line: 1-732-602-3407
PayPal: MrUFO8@hotmail.com

CONTENTS

Publisher and Editor Timothy Green Beckley

CAVEAT

Noun:
1. A Warning Or Proviso Of Specific Stipulations, Conditions Or Limitations.

There are many things you will see and read in this book that seem astonishing.

And truly they are!

It is important to take an open-minded, but critical, view of the material covered within the pages of this work, especially when it comes to the depiction of Nazi UFOs in the air and on the ground. There are those who maintain that these photos have been propagated for propaganda purposes by neo-Nazi groups active around the world or are part of a massive disinformation campaign waged by some possible Fourth Reich positioned at the South Pole. I find it amazing that there are more "good" photos of Nazi UFOs – all looking very "plush and polished," and many done before Photoshop existed – than the UFO groups or even YouTube submitters can supply us with. They look "authentic" but are in many cases staged. The question is: who is putting up the financing to accomplish this task with the hope of possibly fooling the world? Maybe you have an answer. We welcome feedback at mrufo8@hotmail.com

Conspiracy Journal
PRODUCTIONS

01

MY JOURNEY TO THE HOLLOW EARTH
ENTERING THE WORLD OF NAZI UFOS
By Timothy Green Beckley

Back in the mid-1960s, when I first started my, in those days, Lilliputian-sized publishing venture with a modestly priced mimeograph machine, little – if anything – had been written on the Nazi UFO connection. Nor was there any indication that the National Socialist Party led by Hitler held any interest whatsoever in the occult. What we did know is that the mustached dictator had killed an estimated six million Jews during the holocaust and was attempting to spread his Nazi ideology across Europe through the butt of a rifle and the use of aerial bombardment, which sent many a Britisher scurrying into dark underground bunkers for safety's sake.

All that changed with a little samizdat (i.e. pamphlet) issued through a New Age publisher who went only by the name "Michael X."

As far as a lot of people were concerned, Michael X was one of the greatest avatars of the early UFO/New Age movement of the 1950s. He spoke with great articulation and sincerity at many of the well-attended outdoor conventions held annually at Giant Rock, a private landing strip just outside of Joshua Tree in the hot Mohave Desert of Southern California. He spoke calmly and collectedly about the arrival of the silvery spaceships, dubbed flying saucers, explaining how they were piloted by friendly space beings from this solar system and way beyond.

Michael X perceived the Space Brotherhood to be on a mission to elevate our consciousness and invite us to join a cosmic "League of Nations," a federation of spiritually advanced worlds who exist around us and in other dimensions, or so we were told by a group of modern prophets who claimed communications with the starry-eyed Space Brothers who found their way here from nearby as well as remote planets.

I guess you could call Michael X a guru of sorts, though he didn't head a religious cult nor was he looking to attract a fanatical following in the manner of other more self-absorbed "masters" of universal wisdom. No! Michael X was an avatar in the truest sense of the word – an advocate for all humanity.

SECRET EXPLOITS OF ADMIRAL RICHARD E. BYRD

Michael X even went so far as to refuse to reveal his last name so that he didn't become part of a cult of personality. He chose the letter "X" as a reference to the mysteries of our world and the space and time we inhabit. As a result of his secretiveness, there is little known about his background beyond the fact that he was a salesman of some kind before he discovered UFOlogy. I once spoke to Michael X, but the pattern of secrecy continued and I learned nothing more meaningful than I had known before.

The aliens with whom Michael X communed were said to be from Venus, typical of the time period in which he wrote. His contact with them mainly consisted of telepathic voices, and they spoke to him about the secrets of good health and offered a new understanding of science, philosophy and religion that could possibly propel us forward into a New Age of reason and enlightenment. He wrote about what the Venusians had taught him in a series of very concise study guides, perhaps around 25 or so, if I recall correctly. Many of his discourses had to do with holistic health and the aging process, very "time travel-ish" as if they were referring to a "future earth."

But, as it turns out, Michael X's career was not only involved with the sweetness-and-light aspects of the New Age movement. He had also stumbled upon the darker side of UFOlogy – including Nazi-constructed flying discs – which frightened him to the point that he eventually left behind the work he had loved so much. This is a little known secret about Michael X that I don't believe has ever been presented before.

Years after he exited the field, I obtained this information from Dr. Frank E. Stranges, the late author of "Stranger At The Pentagon" and a good friend of Michael X's. Apparently Michael X had run across some UFO-related secret and was deemed to have "gone too far."

As I have noted, Michael X was the first researcher I know of to have mentioned the UFO Nazi connection. He wrote about it in a very sensationalistic work called **WE WANT YOU – IS HITLER ALIVE?** Published in 1969, this was a tiny weight dossier containing information that Michael X considered vital, though he knew that the German vs. extraterrestrial hypothesis/theory he presented would not be a popular one and would doubtlessly draw ample amounts of criticism from those who might think he had turned against his space brother friends.

Need we point out, as we did in our previous work, "Nazi UFO Time Travelers," that Michael's contacts from outer space were decisively Aryan in appearance? If that makes a difference. I always like to point out that these so-called Space Brother-types look like they just walked off the set of an afternoon TV soap opera, so perfectly chiseled are their features. There seemed to be no cultural diversity in space in those days before the evil specter known as the Grays appeared upon the UFO scene.

SECRET EXPLOITS OF ADMIRAL RICHARD E. BYRD

During one of his meditations, a "voice" came to Michael X and gave him a specific place and time to meet for a face-to-face encounter with his supposed alien friends. They promised to reveal some information that had not been disclosed before that would be helpful in the dissemination of his work.

Michael X was sent to a secluded place in the Mohave Desert where he and his contacts could be free of prying eyes. When he arrived, he saw nothing, but remained in his car, waiting. After a while, he saw the glint of something in the sunlight and assumed it was the spacecraft arriving. He began to walk toward where he had seen the light when all of a sudden he sensed terrible danger. He heard an inner voice warning him to flee the scene, and when he looked back he saw one of the men he had intended to meet lowering his rifle, which had been the object that had glittered in the sun, not any ship full of Venusian Space Brothers.

Shortly after, Michael X completely withdrew from the UFO/New Age community and has not been heard from to this day. When I spoke to Michael X in this same time frame, Michael X confirmed the details of the desert escape story, though he refused to elaborate further on anything other than that he was rather unhappy with the fact that he had gone ahead and published the **WE WANT YOU** tract. When asked, I tell people I don't know whether Michael X is still alive or not, but that Michael surely wouldn't mind seeing his works republished for a certain kind of truth seeker to learn from.

WHAT'S BEHIND THE NAZI UFO INVASION OF OUR SKIES?

As indicated, years before anyone else dared touch on the theory that German scientists had stumbled upon a revolutionary form of propulsion and had constructed disc-shaped devices that they had hoped would help them win the war, Michael X freely broached the subject. In conjunction with this issue, Michael also received a warning from the space people to get our tail off the moon and never return – OR ELSE! And if you think David Icke was the first to write about reptilians roaming the earth, guess again, for as early as the mid-1960s Michael X told about the existence of a race of serpents running around inside Rainbow City, located in Antarctica, as part of an inner earth contingent.

Along with the idea of aliens on the moon jealously guarding their territory and the underground race of terrifying, hostile serpents, a great deal has also been written and talked about regarding the belief that Nazi German scientists may have developed working flying saucer technology close to the end of World War II that was later suppressed by the victorious Allies. But one may never have heard the following story, taken from the middle section of "Trilogy Of The Unknown," a volume we published a couple of years back based on material compiled by Michael X.

In this volume, Michael X relates the rise and fall of a German named Karl

SECRET EXPLOITS OF ADMIRAL RICHARD E. BYRD

Michalek, who in 1958, while living in Santiago, Chile, began to write some very unusual articles. He sent his articles to a publication called "Neues Europa," or in English, "New Europe," which was published by Louis Emrich. Emrich printed everything Michalek sent him, and within a short time, Michalek had garnered a large following of readers. The small newspaper had at first printed articles of general interest, but as time passed, Michalek's messages began to dominate the publication. [Michael X is quick to acknowledge the similarity of his own name to Karl Michalek's, which he feels is an unfortunate coincidence that hopefully won't confuse people reading this account.]

Professor de Souza claimed to know about the existence of an underground world in Brazil.

"The German readers were fascinated," Michael X writes, "intensely so."

Just what was stirring up so much excitement? Michalek was calmly announcing in the "New Europe" that he was in positive contact with the governmental heads of the planet Venus. The name of the particular intelligent being from Venus who was acting as Michalek's present contact was "Ase."

"Ase and Michalek are desirous," Michael X writes, "of bringing about everlasting peace and order to our planet Earth. In his series of regularly appearing articles, Karl Michalek presented himself as a sincere, God-fearing man who believes in the almighty power of the Creator. He is against those world groups that are promoting war, which Michalek knows will destroy the planet."

Michalek also authored a book laying out his beliefs called "Michalek: The Prophet of the New Era. Unearthly Forces and the Human Race."

He was not only egocentric enough to call himself a "prophet," he also declared himself to be "the spiritual bearer of this great idealistic world idea" and "the President of the coming majestic government of the World Republic of this Earth." He sent stern warnings to leaders like Nikita Khrushchev and Dwight Eisenhower not to meddle in his Venusians' plans for world conquest or Moscow and Washington would be wiped out.

Michalek also told his followers reading the "New Europe" that the ships from Venus would land on "X-Day," in December of 1958, in Berlin itself, causing great excitement among his loyal throng. Predictably, the day came and went and not a single UFO was seen. Michalek covered his embarrassment by saying that the President of Venus had passed away unexpectedly at the age of 193. Ase, Michalek's contact among the Venusians, was forced to delay the landing maneuver for a short period of time.

"Two years later, Michalek again predicted 'Der Tag X.' This time he stated that it was fixed and irrevocable. The date of the Venus Fleet landing was to be April 21, 1960! Note how X-Day was set for one day after Hitler's birth month and day, April 20.

"April 21st arrived – uneventfully. Again, for some unknown reason, the Venusian UFO fleet had seen fit to stay away. This time, the failure of the spaceships to 'arrive' as Michalek had promised brought forth a storm of protesting letters from readers of the 'New Europe.' Because the predicted Venus landing didn't take place, the curve of Michalek's success has sunk into the negative realm, and Michalek has sunk with it. INTERPOL in Austria takes a very dim view of his claims and is opposed to him. Even Michalek's former staunch supporters, including the disillusioned publisher Louis Emrich, have fallen away."

Hollow Earth But there is more. In 1959, Michalek claimed, "For some time now, I have been the one designated to be President of the highest governmental authority of the coming World Republic. I have been so designated by the power of the Chief Leader of the planet Venus."

Michael X then backtracks to 1945, around two decades to the time in which he was writing. Michael X says that when Hitler was drawing up his last will and testament, he did not name a second Fuhrer to succeed him. He chose Admiral Karl Doenitz as the next President of the Reich, Joseph Goebbels as Reich Chancellor, and Martin Bormann as the Party Minister.

From there, Michael X reasons that Hitler had secretly survived his supposed suicide in Berlin in 1945 and was in fact living in South America. This was easier to believe in 1960, when Hitler would have been in his early 70s. In any case, it was a surviving Hitler who was the true authority that Michalek served, not the disappointing Venusians.

Many in Brazil believe UFOs originate from inside the earth. This is an official photograph of a "bogie" released by the government.

"It is possible," Michael X writes, "that Karl Michalek is in actuality the illegitimate son of Adolph Hitler. Mind you, I say it is 'possible.' I do not claim it is the gospel truth or a proven certainty. No. It's a simple hypothesis and nothing more. So far, Michalek has not 'delivered the goods' in regard to his predictions of UFO landings, and his own broken promises have dubbed him a charlatan, a hoaxer on the grand scale. Those who formerly believed in him now DO NOT."

The point is that Michalek, as a Nazi conspirator and a member of a surviving Hitler's inner circle, did have knowledge of genuine UFOs, but of Nazi design as opposed to true extraterrestrial spacecraft.

"The Michalek story may be part of the Nazis' plans, a preliminary test phase that for some reason, perhaps a good reason, had to be discontinued. If our hypothesis is right, Hitler had the UFO secret. And if we could manage to look in on his Argentine Hideout, we'd no doubt see quite an armada of earth-built UFOs. Not only that. It is also likely we'd find the craft well-armed."

SECRET EXPLOITS OF ADMIRAL RICHARD E. BYRD

Almost impossible to scale, Bernard claimed there is a cleverly disguised entrance to the Inner Earth in the side of this mountain.

So the work of Michael X manages to resonate even in the present time some 50-plus years later, and NOT ONLY in regard to the concept that at least some aspects of the UFO phenomenon might have had their roots in a Nazi space program developed at the end of World War II.

Remarkably, Michael X, as we have seen, is the author/researcher who actually laid the groundwork for a theory that has become increasing popular.

Naturally, as would be expected, there are those who treat the Nazi UFO concept with great suspicion, holding the belief that the German's could NOT have actually had the ability to create a parade of aerial super weapons and time traveling 'space craft' toward the end of the war. They see this belief structure as just so much propaganda by Nazi sympathizers who are holding to the theology that the Fuhrer's strength and might can still be felt to this very day, and that his goal of world conquest lives on in the hearts and minds of those who applaud his grievous exploits. To them a "good lie" is justified if it bolsters Nazi aspirations – past, present or future!

And this may well be the case, as many evildoers roar about freely, their ideals unchecked and unbridled, in an attempt to "pull in" the weak will and those who do not feel the need for "fact checking."

Thus a strong word of warning. . .

BEWARE!

WHICH CAME FIRST? – THE CHICKEN, THE EGG OR THE HOLLOW EARTH?

I say this facetiously of course as there are no chickens inside the hollow earth (none that I know about anyway), though we might think of the earth as a giant egg.

Hard to say when I was introduced to the mystique of the hollow earth. Of

SECRET EXPLOITS OF ADMIRAL RICHARD E. BYRD

course I had read "Journey to the Center of the Earth" by Jules Verne growing up. I suppose it was around the same time I put my career – at fifteen years old – on the line and wrote about Nazi UFOs, thanks to Michael X's seemingly well researched thesis. I started reading Ray Palmer's "Flying Saucers From Other Worlds" magazine I guess around 1961 or 1962 and got a few of the older issues at the Englishtown. New Jersey, Flea Market. My grandmother would shop for fresh fruit and vegetables while I hung out in the used book and magazine racks made up of a bunch of plywood shelves nailed together so that they wobbled a bit when you tried to pull a book down. You could buy almost anything for a quarter, like the books by Major Donald E Keyhoe, who, in the paperback best seller, "Flying Saucers Are Real," contended that the only real explanation for the arrival of the flying saucers was that earth was being visited by beings from other worlds. He wouldn't have it any other way. He didn't even consider the idea that they might be manufactured right under our very noses, on Earth.

In 1959 Palmer broke the news that he had evidence that flying saucers did NOT come from outer space but were the vehicles piloted by a race of beings living inside the center of the earth. I must have thought, plain and simply put, he was crazy. We had been taught in school that at one time centuries ago people thought the earth was flat and that if ships and their crews went too close to the edge they would find themselves either eaten by monsters (an early home for Nessie?) or paddling out into the void of darkness which we now know as outer space.

But Palmer's theory did seem reasonable and I found myself hooked on reading whatever evidence Ray had to offer. One of his sources was a gentleman by the name of Dr. Raymond Bernard, who I found out later on was really born Walter Seigmeister in 1901 to a family of Russian non-observant Jews in New York City. His father was a doctor, which gave him an early interest in health. As a young man he became deeply interested in the works of the Theosophists and Rudolph Steiner's Anthropasophists, especially those works relating to Atlantis and Lemuria.

The only photo known to exist of the somewhat mysterious and always intriguing Dr. Raymond Bernard.

Seigmeister's background is a bit hazy, but from what we can glean he received a B.A. from Columbia University in 1924, and his M.A. and Ph.D. degrees were in education — from New York University (in 1930 and 1932 respectively). His Ph.D. dissertation was, "Theory and Practice of Dr. Rudolf Steiner's Pedagogy."

As I have often recounted, I was busy cranking the handle of my Gestner mimeograph machine when I was but fourteen or maybe fifteen (around 1961-62). I would run ads for free in Palmer's publication; he had a Flying Saucer Club News column where I met and corresponded with the heads of other UFO groups and some of his regular writers who didn't mind sharing their knowledge with us teenage UFOlogists.

This is how I came in contact with Richard Shaver, who insisted there was a vast tunnel system that circled the planet about a mile or more down inside the caverns of Earth. He was a regular contributor to Palmer's various magazines and was as controversial a figure as you could possibly come across in those days.

Shaver insisted that these caverns were populated by a demented race of beings he called the "dero" who had escaped to the inner earth eons ago after the sun began to give off radioactive particles which caused mutations and shortened the lifespan of everyone on the planet. This wasn't exactly the Hollow Earth as we've come to know it from Raymond Bernard and others, but it was, let us say, only a distance of thousands of miles to the core. I suppose you could say this was a good start if you were journeying further inward toward the center of the earth.

All I know is Shaver was sending me letters typed on an old typewriter and punched out on onion skin paper which made them pretty difficult to read. He also was "kind" enough to send me a box full of the best dirt direct from his backyard. He said there were antediluvian paintings embedded on the rocks from thousands of years ago, and if you cut away the rock's surface with a saw they would become all too apparent. My mother didn't appreciate this "sharing of ancient wisdom and knowledge," as the box was usually loaded down with dirt and a few earthworms (which I willingly handed over to my grandfather, who enjoyed a bit of fishing in his leisurely hours).

Dr. Bernard died of pneumonia on September 10, 1965, while searching for a tunnel opening in South America. He had become a bit of an explorer and from time to time would send me updates on his activity. I am almost certain he was also mailing them to other interested parties, but I guess I did feel "special," as Bernard had penned a popular book. "The Hollow Earth" was being heavily advertised and must have sold thousands upon thousands of copies in the heyday of mail order. Bernard, I am almost certain, received zero royalties, and, since the book was apparently in public domain (much like the movie, "Night Of The Living Dead"), it was circulated freely – and I do mean freely as far as its various publishers who put out various "bootlegged" editions were concerned.

DR. BERNARD SPEAKS FROM BEYOND THE GRAVE

It was not unusual for me to receive a communique from Raymond Bernard which was either typed if he were in the city or written by hand if he was out hunting for entrances to the cavern world he believed could possibly go all the way down to the center of the earth. I can't imagine making such a trip, don't even know if it's possible, but Bernard was as energetic as one could be and claimed he had local tribal guides that befriended him and would lead the way.

Says Dr. Bernard: "I arrived in Brazil in 1956 and have been carrying on my research since I met a Theosophical leader who told me about the subterranean cities inhabited by a super race of Atlantean origin that existed in Brazil. He referred me to Professor Henrique Jose de Souza, president of the Brazilian Theosophical Society, at Sao Lourenco in the state of Minas Gerais, who erected a temple dedicated to Agharta, which is the Buddhist name of the subterranean world. Here in Brazil live Theosophists from all parts of the world, all of whom believe in the existence of the subterranean cities.

"Professor de Souza told me that the great English explorer Colonel Fawcett is still alive, living in a subterranean city in the Roncador Mountains of Matto Grosso, where he found the subterranean city of the Atlanteans for which he searched, but is held prisoner lest he reveal the secret of its whereabouts. He was not killed by Indians as is commonly believed.

"Professor de Souza claimed he has visited subterranean cities, including Shamballah, the world capital of the subterranean empire of Agharta. I then went to Matto Grosso to find the subterranean city where Fawcett is claimed to be living with his son Jack, but failed to do so. I then returned to Joinville in the state of Santa Catarina, and there continued my research.

"Just recently two of my explorers returned from entering a tunnel near Ponte Grosse in the state of Parana. One of them had recently entered alone and spent five days in the underworld city there. It had about 50 inhabitants plus children. The fruit orchards were recently planted, and the inhabitants received fruit from another subterranean city. During the last visit, the two explorers were met at the entrance of the tunnel by a guardian and the chief of the city, who told them that they should return in two years when the fruit trees will start to bear, but cannot enter now."

Through my own research, I found out that the concept of an inner earth is more common in Brazil than one might think. The local Macuxi Indians who live along the Amazon say there is a whole new world waiting to be explored, a place where living beings inhabit the depths of our planet, a place that cultures and ancient civilizations knew existed, and that it still exists today.

According to local accounts, numerous indigenous peoples living in the Amazon, in countries like Brazil, Guyana and Venezuela, hold to their oral traditions and legends that say they are the descendants of the children of the Sun, the creator of fire and protective of the "inner Earth."

SECRET EXPLOITS OF ADMIRAL RICHARD E. BYRD

Sentries from the Macuxies tribe were said to guard entrances to the Hollow Earth.

It is said that the Macuxies entered a cavern and traveled 13 to 15 days until they reached the interior. It is there, "on the other side of the world, in the inner Earth," where giant creatures that are about 3-4 meters high are said to be living.

According to legend, the Macuxies were given the task of monitoring outside the entrance and preventing outsiders from entering the "hollow Earth." Those legends say Macuxi people enter the mysterious cave for three days, but only giants can descend the stairs, which measure about 80 centimeters for each step. After the third day, they leave behind their torches and continue their journey "inside" Earth, which is illuminated by the lights that were already present in the caves. Giant lanterns, the size of a watermelon, shining like the sun. After 4-5 days of travel, those inside the cave lose weight and body mass, allowing them to move much faster.

The legends of the Macuxi say that after five days inside the caverns, they would encounter huge caverns whose roofs could not be seen. In one of the chambers of the cave system, there are four objects "like the sun," which are impossible to watch and whose purpose is unknown to the Macuxi village. Within the Earth, there are places where trees are able to grow food. The Macuxi say cajúes fruits like, oak, mangos, bananas and some smaller plants were apparent 6-7 days into their journey. The farther the Macuxi people moved into the Earth, the larger

11

the areas of vegetation they observed. But not all areas are of a green and prosperous color. The Macuxi people say that some places are extremely dangerous and should be avoided, such as those with boiling stone and streams "azoge."

According to ZonNews, who printed the story initially: "Macuxi Oral traditions continue and say that after going through these giant caverns, they had to move carefully as the mysterious 'air' can cause people to 'fly or float' around. Continuing their journey, they reached a place within the Earth where the Giants lived. There, the Macuxi explorers ate food from the giants, such as apples the size of human heads, grapes the size of a human fist, and delicious, giant fish captured by the giants were given as gifts to the Macuxi.

"After stocking up with the offered giant food, Macuxi explorers return 'home' to the world 'outside,' helped by the giants of the inner world. It is said that the Macuxi are the 'guardians' of the underworld, guarding the entrance to the Inner Earth, which is full of incredible power and wealth."

Dr. Bernard, as it turned out, had many accounts to share:

"An elderly man living in Joinville once told me that he had visited a tunnel near Concepiao in the state of Sao Paulo, and saw in the distance a marvelous subterranean city with vehicles darting back and forth, evidently traveling through tunnels from one subterranean city to another.

****

Similarly: "Although the following report requires conformation, it was told to me by an explorer named N.C. who said that he had visited a tunnel near Rio Casdor and had met a beautiful young woman appearing to be 20 years of age. She spoke to him in Portuguese and said that she was 2,500 years of age. He also met a bearded subterranean man. Still another explorer named D.O., visited this same tunnel and saw a child inside who fled upon seeing him. Also as he once lay in front of the tunnel opening, a man with a beard and long hair passed over him and entered."

Bernard confided in me that entrances to the inner/hollow earth could be found not only in Brazil and at the North and South Poles but in other countries as well.

"Apparently such tunnels into the subsurface exist elsewhere in the world besides Brazil. In fact one letter on file with us comes from Prof. W. Wiers of Mexico, who tells us that he knew Prof. Schwartz, who had made a long study of cave problems, starting when he was 15 years old in Germany.

"According to Prof. Wiers, just before the beginning of the Second World War, both the Axis and Allied powers were interested in using various caves as supply bases and for many military applications.

"Prof. Schwartz at one time had stated that he knew of a Nazi who had come upon an 'enormous circular pit' (in Brazil? – Branton) whose sides dropped straight down for a good 1200 feet. Trees could be seen growing tall and straight below. Eagles soared around, and then dived to the center of the bottom, apparently to eat something. Since the sides were dangerously steep, the Nazi had to content himself with using binoculars instead of descending into this world himself.

"Returning later with others, he eventually discovered a similar but much narrower bore, or shaft, not far from the first, which was so big that it could not be hidden in any way. Not having cable or apparatus with which to let down a man in the seemingly bottomless shaft, they let down a pencil attached to a rope. To their surprise, the cord, when drawn back up, was found to be cut clean, as with a knife, or scissors – and the pencil was gone. Of course they all resolved to come back to study this pit further but the war prevented their doing so.

"The location of this shaft is supposedly in northern Guatemala. Near the place is a witch doctor, friendly to Prof. Schwartz, who assured the professor that there is a secret passage, closed by a revolving rock door, which goes to the still enormous chamber which is still below the vast roof cave-in seen from above."

Shortly before his death from a respiratory disorder, Bernard declared: "After a 32-year search through 20 countries of Central and South America, I at last found what I sought – THE SUBTERRANEAN CITIES OF THE ATLANTEANS, which exist mostly in Santa Catarina, Brazil, and especially in the Joinville area. Luminous flying saucers were seen to rise from a subterranean city of small men, and from other subterranean cities of tall Atlanteans. The world will learn that FLYING SAUCERS ARE OF SUBTERRANEAN ORIGIN!"

While I cannot prove this, I have heard rumors to the effect that Raymond Bernard had been poisoned because he dared to reveal the truth about this monumental discovery – perhaps the most important of all time. Others suggested that his diet was what did him in eventually as he is said to have existed solely on fruits from the jungle.

His final and most popular book was the *"The Hollow Earth."* He died of pneumonia on September 10, 1965, while searching the tunnel openings to the interior of the Earth in South America. He was an individual who was not afraid to explore well beyond the confines of the "established convention," and the spirit of his controversial research lives on . . .

SUGGESTED READING

TRILOGY OF THE UNKNOWN – A CONSPIRACY READER: EXPOSING

THE DARK SIDE OF UFO RESEARCH by Michael X

THE HOLLOW EARTH by Dr. Raymond Bernard

CHILLING TALES OF THE SHAVER MYSTERY edited by Tim Beckley and Wm Kern

"HIDDEN WORLD" SERIES by Raymond Palmer (Sixteen Updated Editions by Tim Beckley's Inner Light - Global Communications)

02

MICAH HANKS

Author, Podcaster, Musician, Adventurer.

Follow me online at
micahhanks.com

Dark Secrets Below the Ice: The Truth Behind Antarctica's 'Nazi UFO Base' Conspiracy
By Micah Hanks

It's one of the most famous conspiracies associated with the end of the Second World War: that a group of Nazis escaped to Antarctica, where they had a secret base established to aid in the furtherance of their top secret flying saucer development program.

Such tales have been the stuff of legends for decades now, and the persistence of rumors like these offer an alternative to popular theories about alien visitors that remain a hallmark of modern UFO lore.

This idea has had renewed attention during the last few years, thanks to widespread attention given to a 2006 discovery by Ohio State University scientists, who actually did find some variety of "gravitation anomaly" located below Wilkes Land, Antarctica. Even more recently, tabloids like *The Mirror* have run with stories that cite speculation that the "anomaly" could actually be the long-sought "secret Nazi UFO base" in question.

It should be noted, firstly, that there is some legitimacy to the idea of a Nazi presence in Antarctica during the years leading up to World War II. In fact, the continent's strategic importance culminated in an expedition by Germany that occurred between 1938 and 1939. With little doubt, this fact remains a contributing factor in the beliefs that Nazis may have even tried to establish a more permanent stronghold at the South Pole.

It is also well known that a variety of advanced aircraft had been designed by the Germans toward the end of the war, with further allegations that some of these were said to resemble flying saucers. If so, there have never been any reports or documents made public that would indicate the veracity of claims about "saucers" the Nazis built.

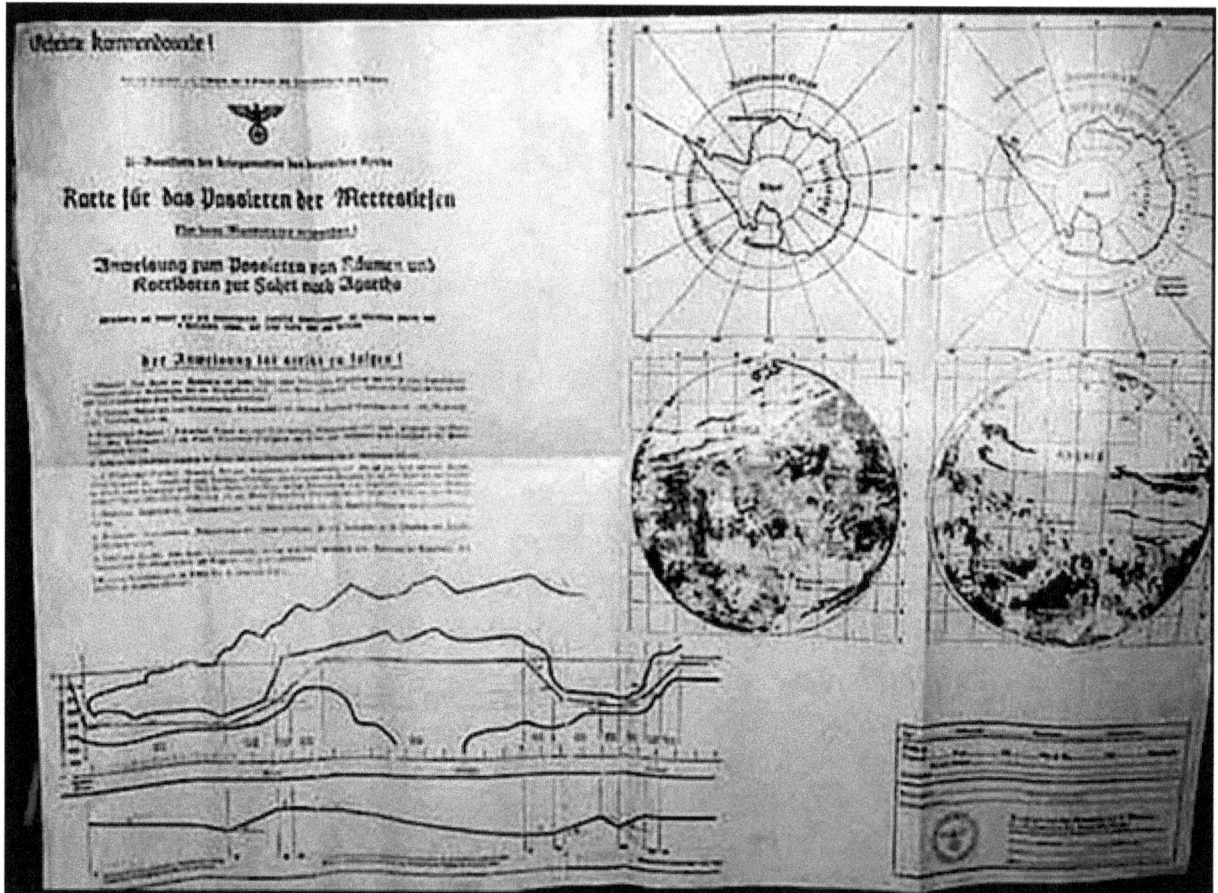

Maps to the Inner Earth are said to exist — but how real are they?

In large part, the crux of the entire Nazi UFO affair has long remained centered around a fabled device known as *Die Glocke*, or "the bell", a supposed Nazi weapons project that was rumored to have been anything from some kind of experimental antigravity device, to a special anti-aircraft weapon. Yet again (and despite this author's own pursuit of leads on this subject for a number of years), a damning lack of good source material turns up in relation to *Die Glocke*, at least outside of alternative or "fringe" literature, that can help support the case that such a device ever existed.

So far, none of this points to any conclusive evidence of a Nazi base located in Antarctica. So what, apart from the expeditions carried out by Germany during the 1930s, might serve as the genesis of these legends about a "Nazi UFO Base" in the southernmost Polar Regions?

SECRET EXPLOITS OF ADMIRAL RICHARD E. BYRD

BEGINNINGS: OPERATION HIGHJUMP (1946-47)

This notion actually has less to do with anything the Nazis themselves did, and instead appears to stem from a series of cryptic comments made by Rear Admiral Richard E. Byrd during an interview with International News Service correspondent Lee van Atta, which took place aboard the USS Mount Olympus in 1947. The interview was said to have appeared in the Wednesday, March 5, 1947 edition of a Chilean newspaper *El Mercurio*.

Below is the relevant portion of the interview, in which Byrd makes some rather startling allusions to "flying objects":

Adm. Byrd declared today that it was imperative for the United States to initiate immediate defense measures against hostile regions. The admiral further stated that he didn't want to frighten anyone unduly but that it was a bitter reality that in case of a new war the continental United States would be attacked by flying objects which could fly from pole to pole at incredible speeds. Admiral Byrd repeated the above points of view, resulting from his personal knowledge gathered both at the north and south poles, before a news conference held for International News Service.

As one can see, such wording easily lends itself to the idea of a connection between the Nazi UFO mythos, and something going on at the South Pole. So based on the presumption that the statements above, and the *Mercurio* article itself were indeed legitimate, one can only guess what kind of perceived threat prompted Byrd to make such claims during the interview in question. Had some kind of danger actually existed in the southernmost extremities of Antarctica just after World War II? If so, what was the nature of this threat, and could it have dealt with carry-overs from Nazi Germany, as some UFO researchers have already speculated over the years?

Some would maintain that the best evidence for the legitimacy of Byrd's statements, and their UFOlogical interpretation, actually has to do with Byrd's reasons for visiting Antarctica in the first place. Byrd had been tasked with leading the ill-fated Operation Highjump, which occurred between late 1946 and early 1947, and involved an extremely heavy military presence. Hence, some in UFO circles have gone so far as to suggest that Byrd's "Operation Highjump" represented a secret battle between U.S. forces and a group of secret Antarctic residents with advanced Nazi UFO technologies. After all, what else might have sent Byrd and his scores of ships and aircraft packing so quickly after embarking upon this extensive, and extremely well-funded military expedition? This theory, of course, would also seem to explain the "flying objects which could fly from pole to pole at incredible speeds" that Byrd had so cryptically warned us of... right?

To the contrary, it seems that what Byrd was actually discussing was the threat of an enemy nation getting to Antarctica, and establishing military

bases *before the Americans did so.* In fact, although details about it remained undisclosed for many years, the establishment of strategic bases had been *precisely* what the American presence during Operation Highjump had aimed to do.

Hence, rather than bumping into secret Nazi bases and their armaments while there, Byrd and his company encountered a far more formidable enemy: mother nature.

The brutal conditions during the winter in question had been causing a variety of issues, particularly with aircraft, by late January 1947. In one dramatic instance, a sudden downwind managed to sweep a helicopter in mid-takeoff directly into the ocean water, leaving a narrow window of opportunity for the pilot to escape and be rescued. There were plenty of other situations, however, where the servicemen involved weren't as lucky; complications resulting from extreme weather conditions led to the loss of several lives during the short period that Operation Highjump was underway.

Needless to say, the unnecessary loss of human life is never a thing to be desired, and Operation Highjump was terminated in February 1947, on account of the worsening weather.

Returning again to Byrd's cryptic statements given to *El Murcurio*, there wouldn't necessarily need to have been enemy aircraft present at the time of Op-

SECRET EXPLOITS OF ADMIRAL RICHARD E. BYRD

eration Highjump to validate the Byrd's commentary. By the end of WWII, experimental jet engines were already in development, and within a few short years, planes that incorporated such designs would revolutionize both military and commercial aircraft. With little doubt, Admiral Byrd knew this, and spoke of the expectation that any military with a permanent presence at the South Pole might be able to use this strategic location to launch aircraft that could reach any place on Earth within just a few short hours; a "bitter reality" indeed.

'FLYING OBJECTS,' NAZI UFO TECH OR EXAGGERATIONS?

There is another factor worthy of consideration here, which has to do with whether Byrd's statements about lightning fast "flying objects" might have been somewhat exaggerated, too. Antarctic explorer Paul Siple noted of the famous *Mercurio* interview that the reporters aboard the USS Mount Olympus had overblown claims from Byrd's earlier expeditions in the region, pertaining to the so-called "Bungers Oasis," a lake area found to have uniquely warm temperatures (around 30 degrees) and a variety of algae growing within. Byrd later described the location as a "land of blue and green lakes and brown hills in an otherwise limitless expanse of ice," and that his crew had "seemed to have dropped out of the twentieth century into a landscape of thousands of years ago when land was just starting to emerge from one of the great ice ages." There were, of course, no reports of mammoths or flying saucers mentioned in conjunction with this, although Byrd would later call the discovery "by far the most important, so far as the public interest was concerned of the expedition."

Nonetheless, Siple notes:

"...[T]he eleven press representatives aboard the USS Mount Olympus had fired off dispatches to the outside world describing

Admiral Byrd set to explore at the pole.

SECRET EXPLOITS OF ADMIRAL RICHARD E. BYRD

Helicopter used during Project Highjump.

Ice free valley explored by Admiral Richard E. Byrd.

Micah Hanks prepares to broadcast another episode of "The Grailien Report."

the oasis as a 'Shangri-La' and implying that it was warmed by a mysterious source of heat and might be supporting vegetation."

This no doubt helped fuel additional fringe claims associated with Byrd's expeditions: namely, that they had discovered a habitable region at the South Pole, wherein a cavernous entry point into the Earth led them to meet residents who existed below ground. Offering an alternate theory about the origin of flying saucers, this group of "Hollow Earth Dwellers" further told Byrd that the mysterious flying saucers had actually belonged to them, a fanciful story presented in a bogus document long claimed to have been a "secret diary" that Byrd kept during his Antarctic explorations.

Taken into context, the embellishment of such details by the press could easily have served as the root of claims about not only a prehistoric "oasis" at the South Pole, but also the "flying craft" and, eventually, a secret Nazi base that would appear amidst conspiracy theories for years to come.

Again, it seems likely that Byrd had been making a general statement about the potential uses of enemy aircraft during the coming decades, in the sense that a hostile nation, should they ever establish a base at one of the poles, might use the area as a centralized point for launching attacks against the US mainland. Looking further back, Byrd had previously suggested that the US might seek to establish such a base at the North Pole as well; hence, it seems clear that he viewed the polar extremities as advantageous locations.

Finally, Byrd's acknowledgement that, "in the case of a new war," seems to further indicate that his statements dealt not with any existing menace, but instead with the potential for a future threat by an enemy nation. With World War II still fresh on people's minds, many at the time shared concerns such as these.

All fantastic speculation aside, what we are left with is very little ground for believing that Operation Highjump prematurely ended due to the presence of hidden subterranean races, attacks by woolly mammoths, or even "flying objects" the likes of Nazi UFOs. Few would argue, however, that the various grains of truth pertaining to Byrd's historic operations have seeded themselves in the fertile grounds of myth and speculation, taking on an all new—and utterly fascinating—life of their own throughout the last several decades.

Courtesy
http://www.micahhanks.com/

THE UNVARNISHED TRUTH ABOUT
INVESTIGATOR TIM CRIDLAND

Were you to say "there is nothing new under the sun," you would be absolutely incorrect. The following is a breaking news report regarding Admiral Byrd's expedition that is worthy of being given major press coverage on CNN and other media outlets – and NO it is NOT fake news, but is based upon a lengthy, ongoing investigation by a Vegas-based researcher. It is an investigation that highlights the fact that, even though it is more than a half century since Byrd flew to the South Pole – and possibly well beyond! – that it is still possible to uncover further facts and documentation which show that Admiral Byrd's expedition was more "involved" than it was purported to be.

Tim Cridland has had an interest in the strange and the unusual from an early age. In the late 1980s through the early 1990s he published a 'zine called "Off The Deep End," which he described as "the world's first punk/Fortean/Discordian/weird science/conspiracy 'zine."

In the 1990s he took a break from writing to become a strange and unusual performer – first as one of the original members of the Jim Rose Circus Sideshow and then with his own show.

His "Wild Talent" of pain control and mind over matter have been verified by scientists around the world. He has been profiled on TV shows, including "48 Hours with Dan Rather," "Ripley's TV" and "Stan Lee's Superhumans."

He has done research for various authors, including Jim Keith ("Casebook on Alternative Three" and other books), Adam Gorightly ("Caught in the Crossfire"), and Jim Hogshire ("Grossed Out Surgeon")

He is the co-author of "Weird Las Vegas and Nevada" and "Circus of the Scars," as well as having essays published in "Mysteries of Mount Shasta" and "Electricity of the Mind: Anomalist 14."

You can find more of his writings at OTDEZine.blogspot.com

BadSkeptic.blogspot.com

Zamora.blogspot.com

DecadentDallas.blogspot.com

Tim Cridland does not believe anything he reads and even less of what he writes.

03

HAS THE MYSTERIOUS HOLE AT THE POLE BEEN PHOTOGRAPHED?
By Tim Cridland

The following article will be hard to comprehend if the reader lacks familiarity with the Hollow Earth theory. The theory, in a nutshell, is that the Earth is hollow with large openings at the North and South Poles. The interior is lit by a small red "central sun" that keeps the climate at a constant tropical temperature. The inhabitants walk along the inner crust, held in place by the force of gravity. They are probably the pilots of flying saucers. The most widely available book on the subject is "The Hollow Earth," by Raymond Bernard. You are urged to read this book if you are unfamiliar with the subject.

HOLE-AT-THE-POLE PHOTOGRAPHS: AN OVERVIEW

The question most often asked by the uninitiated when discussing the Hollow Earth theory: "If there are holes at the poles, why aren't there any satellite photos of them?"

The usual response is to pull out the photos uncovered by Ray Palmer in the June 1970 issue of "Flying Saucers Magazine." Palmer, the man that some claim was responsible for starting the public's obsession with flying saucers, had started the modern-day Hollow Earth movement in an earlier issue of the magazine. Drawing on accounts of Admiral Byrd's polar flights as reported in the then-recently published "Worlds Beyond the Poles," by Amadeo F. Giannini, Palmer realized that Byrd's alleged reports of tropical conditions at the polar area fit in with conjectures about an inner world that were popular in the 19th century just as easily with Giannini's much more bizarre extended-space theory.

Palmer, upon finding the photo taken by the ESSA-7 satellite on November 23, 1968, declared "The North Pole photo, lacking clouds in the polar area, therefore reveals the surface of the planet. Although surrounding the polar area, and north of such areas as the North American continent and Greenland and the Asian continent, we can see the ice fields of the eight-foot thick ice . . . (in the photo) we do not see any ice fields in a large circular area directly at the geographic pole. Instead, we see – THE HOLE!"

SECRET EXPLOITS OF ADMIRAL RICHARD E. BYRD

There have been other satellite photos that are claimed to show a polar void, but not many from a polar orbit. Polar photos aren't very easy to find; there aren't many satellites in polar orbits, so this isn't that surprising. (Palmer claims that early troubles with polar-orbit satellites were due to miscalculations caused by the hole.) The polar photos that I've managed to find fall into four categories: 1. Jagged-edged un-photographed areas; 2. Fade to black night areas; 3. Complete cloud-cover; 4. Infrared and microwave. Palmer's "Flying Saucers" cover is an example of the first kind of photo. Although Palmer says that this is a photo of "the Hole," this is clearly not the case. It has been shown that this a composite photo-mosaic made from many satellite passes. This explains why the Earth is lit from all around. If this had been a single half, the globe would be dark; the half that is experiencing night. The dark area at the polar region has been explained as the 24-hour night that is experienced in the high northern latitudes in the winter months. I maintain that both of these interpretations are at odds with the facts.

This photo clearly does not show the Hole-at-the-Pole. According to Hollow Earth tradition, the interior of the Earth is illuminated by a small red "central sun." A photo taken directly above the pole, without cloud cover, should show the central sun shining brightly. This would seem to validate the polar-night explanation – if it weren't for some glaring inconsistencies.

In Flora Benton's book, "Hollow Earth at the End Time," she points out that the ESSA-7 November 23rd photo could not have been taken on the claimed date "because it shows light reaching to approximately 76 degrees latitude. The North Cape of Norway, at 71 degrees, is in darkness for two months of every year, and these months would fall before and after December 22nd." A complete polar night photo would show a twilight area and a slow progression into the blackness of night, caused by the refraction of sunlight in the Earth's atmosphere. This is evident in another photo that has been brought forth to boost the Hollow Earth position. This is clearly how a polar night should look.

To understand Palmer's "Hole" photo we must look at another photo that to my knowledge has never been published before. This photos shows a jagged black area at the northern pole that, at one point, juts outward from a circular pattern. Clearly this is not a hole, unless a chunk of the polar rim has broken off and fallen into the Earth's interior. The dark area is also not polar night, unless there were some very extreme temperature inversions in the area of the jagged portion.

It becomes obvious what is happening in these photos: the U.S. government is not photographing sections of the polar area. The question is raised: why? The implication: perhaps they don't want you to see the light from the central sun.

The next type of polar photo (type 3) that I've run across shows the polar area, fully lit but obscured by cloud cover. Palmer claims that the almost constant cloud cover is the reason that there are so few "Hole" shots. He even goes so far as to quote from the Bible to boost his position: Job 26:7,8. "He it was who spread the north above the void, and poised the Earth on nothingness. He fastens up the waters in his clouds – the mists do not tear apart under their weight."

This constant cloud cover can be easily understood from the Hollow Earth viewpoint; if the hollow interior of the Earth is temperate, as is claimed in Hollow Earth tradition, then the subzero air of the outer world meeting the almost tropical inner air would naturally form a dense mist.

When Palmer was writing, infrared satellite photography was nonexistent. Infrared photography would easily penetrate the clouds because it records heat, not light. Thus, if an infrared camera were to take a photo of the polar area from space, one would expect to see a hot area at the pole. Alas, this isn't what the first infrared polar shots show. What we do see is the aurora borealis surrounding the poles. Some of these photos show some unusual aurora formations, such as the time the aurora ring formed an O-shape with some bright concentrated areas.

Of course these photos don't rule out a Hollow Earth. Being government photos, if the government had photographed anything that they didn't want you to see, they would doctor the photos, as it appears happened with the earlier photos. Nonetheless, infrared photos haven't helped the Hollow Earth position either – that is, until now.

HOLE IN OZONE OVER SOUTH POLE WORRIES SCIENTISTS

A massive hole, initially reported by British scientists in March 1985, has been discovered in the ozone above the South Pole. This hole in the upper atmosphere, appearing each September and October, should be letting in hazardous cosmic rays in the south polar area. Atmospheric scientists are concerned that the hole may be growing in size, potentially threatening populated areas (shades of Alternative 3!)

"The Antarctic hole appears at the end of winter . . . by the end of November, the ozone, at altitudes of eight to sixteen miles, recovers. Each year, though, the hole has expanded, in 1985 reaching a size equivalent to the area of the United States." Infrared photos of the ozone hole look remarkably like what one would expect an infrared Hollow Earth photo to look like.

The cause of the hole is not yet understood. Theories of the cause of the ozone void range from volcanic particles and changes in solar activity to releases of chlorine and bromine gasses. "Some climate experts believe that a change in the motions of waves in cyclones in the upper atmosphere might cause the hole. For example, an upwelling of air over the pole could push aside the layer of the stratosphere containing the most ozone, replacing it with low ozone air from lower altitudes . . . . Current climate models do not produce this effect."

"Off The Deep End" suggests that the cause of the hole in the atmosphere

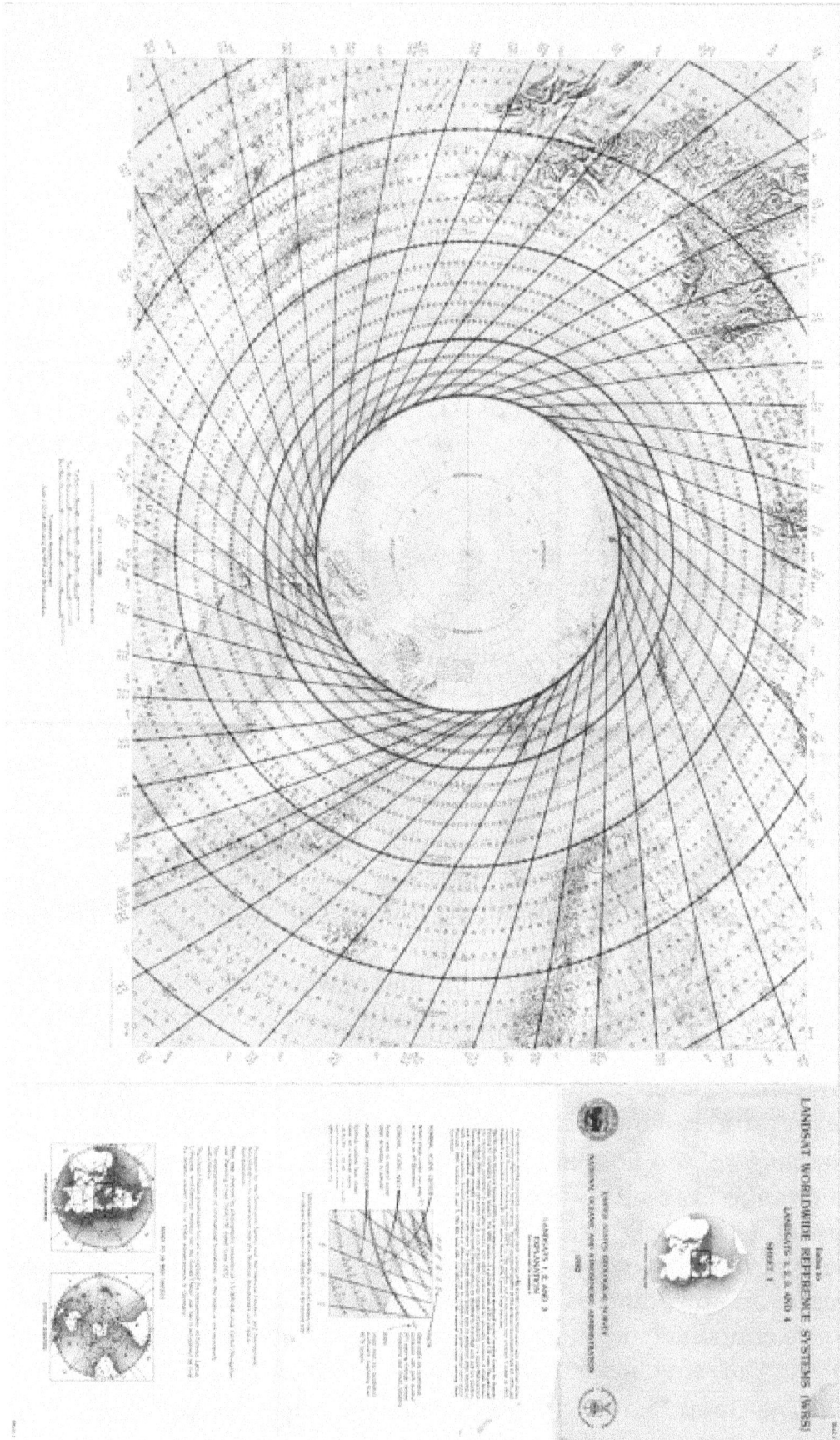

THE VIEW FROM ABOVE

Meteorologists are, among other things, professional watchers of clouds, reading present and future weather partly from the development of different cloud types — and partly from thousands of temperature, wind velocity, pressure, and humidity measurements. The earth-orbiting satellites operated by NOAA's National Environmental Satellite Service play an important part in these activities, providing a vantage point in space for National Weather Service meteorologists on the ground.

□ A three-part, computer-assembled mosaic of the world's cloud cover, seen by satellite cameras in space, is combined with other data to depict global weather.

C_H, C_M and C_L are the World Meteorological Organization code symbols for high, middle, and low clouds. Each cloud type is assigned a number. Refer to the National Weather Service Observing Handbook No. 1 for a complete explanation.

Most of the photographs in this chart appear in the **International Cloud Atlas**, produced by the World Meteorological Organization, and are used with the kind permission of the copyright owners shown below; parenthetic numerals show Atlas plate numbers, other numerals refer to consecutive appearance in this chart.

1 (147), 8 (61), 9 (143), 10 (73), 13 (48B), 23 (23), 25 (6), 26 (13): photographs by A. J. Aalders, copyright Royal Netherlands Meteorological Institute, De Bilt / 2 (219), 3 (133), 4 (123), 5 (119), 7 (199), 11 (80), 12 (153), 14 (58), 15 (158), 16 (103), 17 (106), 20 (30), 22 (26): copyright the World Meteorological Organization, Geneva / 6 (197): copyright the Institute of Theoretical Astrophysics, University of Oslo, Oslo 3 / 18 (89): copyright T. Bergeron, Meteorologista Institutionen, Upsala, Sweden / 19 ( ): NOAA photo by Roger Jensen / 21 ( ): NOAA photo by John Roseborough / 24 (21): copyright Météorologie Nationale — Paris, France.

For sale by the Superintendent of Documents, U.S. Government Printing Office, Washington,

Tim Cridland
A.K.A.
Zamora The Torture King

UNRAVELING THE SECRETS
W.M Mott & Tim Swartz

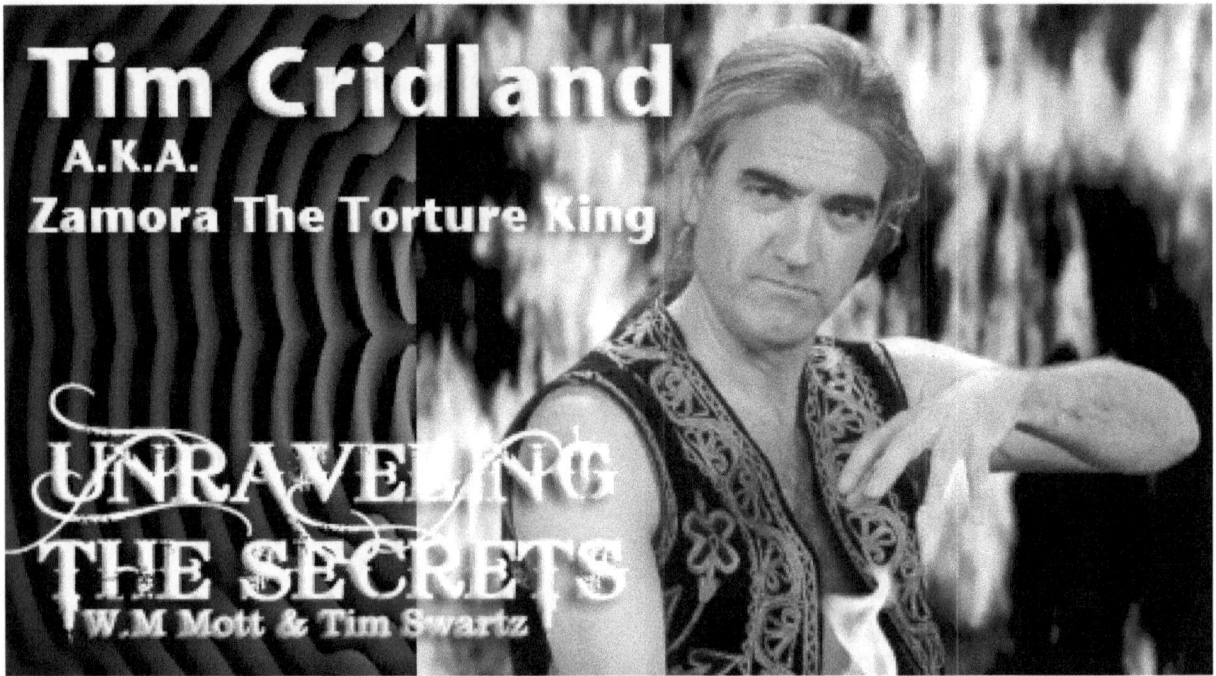

A man for all reasons:
The enigmatic
Tim Cridland.

results directly from the hole-at-the-pole directly below it. The upwelling of air could come from directly underneath via the inner atmosphere. The upwelling is most probably caused by an interaction of the inner and outer atmospheres during the seasonal changes.

Another kind of polar photograph is the microwave photo. There exists an image of Antarctica produced by an ESMR (Electronically Scanning Microwave Radiometer) onboard the Nimbus 5 satellite. The ESMR device measures microwave radiation from the Earth's surface, using a meter-square scanner and a sensitive 1.55 cm wavelength receiver. As the scanner sweeps from side to side, an onboard computer halts it for a fraction of a second, takes measurement, and resumes the sweep. Each line of the image is made up of 78 such stops, completed every four seconds. At the wavelength used by ESMR, radiation penetrates the cloud cover and allows the surface brightness to be measured. The result is a map-like image recording neither heat nor light, but a quality known as "surface brightness temperature" – the relationship between the physical temperature of the target and the rate at which it gives off energy in the 1.55 cm band of the spectrum.

The brightness temperature variations from dark blue to magenta are not yet fully understood. Perhaps the reason that many scientists are confused by polar photos is because they do not allow for a Hollow Earth in their cosmos.

Polar photos haven't hurt the Hollow Earth position at all, because each new photo demonstrates that the poles are, indeed, shrouded in mystery.

MORE HOLLOW EARTH INFO

Now and then people write to me and say "Stop printing all that Hollow Earth stuff. It's just ridiculous." Well, what's the use of calling my zine "Off The Deep End" if I can't print Hollow Earth stuff? Besides, I've got a torch to carry, as "The Hollow Hassle" hasn't published in years.

The February 22, 1993, issue of "TIME" has this to say about seismic studies of the shockwave produced by a recent nuclear blast: "Studies of the shockwave given off by the Chinese 0.66 megaton nuclear test have revealed a 'continent' 3,200 km underground." The article goes on to say that the "continent" is used loosely. Apparently, they do not want us to confuse our inner and outer continents, but it then goes on to say: "What two scientists at the U.S. Geological Survey found was a region 320 km across and 130 km deep that is denser than the surrounding regions. The implication: the core-mantle boundary may be as complex as the Earth's surface."

In the National Oceanic and Atmospheric Administration publication entitled "Clouds" (NOAA/PA 71012), there is a most interesting set of photographs. Under the heading "The View From Above," there are three photographs of the Earth. One of the northern hemisphere, one of the southern hemisphere, and one of the equator. The implication of the text that accompanies these photos is that they can be combined to create an image of the whole Earth.

The problem is that the images of both Poles show a black space where cloud cover should be. According to debunkers, this blackness is simply how a satellite mosaic shows the 24-hour night at the Poles. The problem with this is that there can never be night at both Poles at the same time. Yet this is what seems to be claimed in the text. Something is wrong here.

Follow The Author On FaceBook

www.facebook.com/ZamoraTKing<http://www.facebook.com/ZamoraTKing>

Tim Cridland | Facebook<http://www.facebook.com/ZamoraTKing>

www.facebook.com

Tim Cridland is on Facebook. Join Facebook to connect with Tim Cridland and others you may know.

Admiral Richard E. Byrd

04

Admiral Byrd: Secret Diaries, Secret Societies and the JFK Assassination
By Tim Cridland
©Tim Cridland 2016

Admiral Richard Byrd flew beyond the poles into the Hollow Earth – or so the story goes.

The very successful print advertisement for the book "*The Hollow Earth*" shows an illustration of the legendary explorer with the copy saying, "The Underground World of Supermen Discovered by Admiral Byrd... Under the North Pole...and Kept Secret by the U.S. Government!"

Raymond Bernard, a pseudonym for Walter Siegmeister, author of *The Hollow Earth*, owed a debt to Raymond Palmer, as most of Bernard's information about Byrd's alleged Inner Earth journey was taken straight from Palmer's magazine "*Flying Saucers*."

Palmer, in turn, acquired his information about Byrd from a strange book called "*Beyond the Poles*" by Amadeo F. Giannini, published by Vantage Press in 1959.

Vantage was what was known as a vanity press; they would publish any author – as long as said author was willing to pay them. It was the last refuge for often-rejected manuscripts; an old style of self-publishing, which included the delusion that the book had a "real" publisher. When a magazine editor received a vanity-press book for review, it would most likely go straight into the waste basket.

But Giannini had luck on his side. Ray Palmer was someone who, while working for the science-fiction magazine "*Amazing Stories*," had pulled a letter out of the waste basket and created a publishing sensation. This was the infamous Shaver Mystery, tales about an underground race that had much in common with Hollow Earth lore, which were presented as fact and polarized science-fiction fandom.

"*Beyond the Poles*" was not a Hollow Earth book. Giannini's theory was far stranger than that. It concerned the physical continuation of space. But Giannini's book had the information about Byrd's alleged strange experiences in the polar areas. Palmer took that, combined it with information from forgotten Hollow Earth books and the aforementioned Shaver Mystery, added flying saucers to the mix and created a new curiosity for his readers. It was a hit, and flying saucers from inside the Earth became a frequent topic of his magazine.

Over the years, Giannini's and Palmer's claims about Byrd's experiences have been called into question – there were problems with some of the dates and quotes – but it does seem that there was something strange going on.

Byrd's polar explorations intersect with rumors of secret societies and have a surprising connection to the assassination of John F. Kennedy. Even the stories about missing diaries, dubious as they may seem, may have some inescapable truth to them.

BYRD AIMS AT THE POLES

Byrd had tried to fly to the North Pole with aid from the U.S. Navy. After several unsuccessful efforts, government sponsorship was no longer available.

Determined, he pressed on and acquired private investors. He successfully solicited funds from a list of names that reads like a Who's Who of the power elite: Ford, Rockefeller, among others.

Byrd had enjoyed being a public figure from an early age, and his polar quest was turning him into a celebrity. The public adoration, along with the need to show his patrons that their investments were producing results, may have caused him to embellish his achievements.

On May 9, 1926, after many setbacks, pilot Floyd Bennett, with Byrd navigating, set out toward the North Pole. They radioed back that they had made it and returned heroes.

Even to this day, academics are still debating as to whether they actually reached the North Pole or if Byrd cooked the logbooks. The accusations were private at first, but some openly wondered how they could have made the claimed distance in the arctic conditions in the time that they were in the air. Of course, if the geography was different than what was thought, it could explain the discrepancy.

True or not, the apparent success of the mission snowballed Byrd's celebrity status and his ego while simultaneously generating interest from wealthy investors to bankroll his next project –   flying over the South Pole. One of those investors would be his cousin, David Harold "Dry Hole" Byrd, who had just recently overcome his nickname by becoming a Texas oil millionaire.

Byrd's initial South Pole expeditions were not only privately funded but attracted a slew of adventure-hungry volunteers. This would lead to trouble.

Admiral Byrd and American icon
Charles Lindbergh.

Men look out the fifth floor window of the Texas State School
Book Depository building shortly after the assassination of
President John F. Kennedy on November 22, 1963. Harold Byrd
had owned the building since 1939.

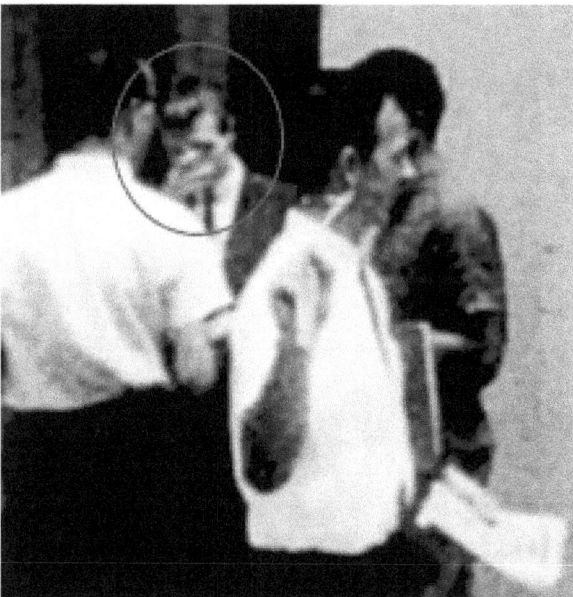

Thomas Beckham in the background while Lee Harvey Oswald
hands out Fair Play for Cuba leaflets

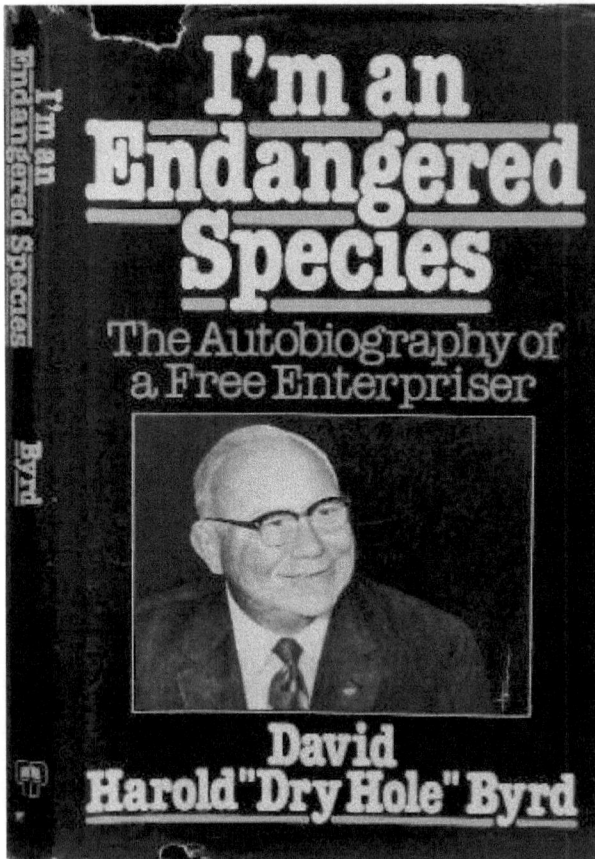

Always thought of as a "straight shooter" Admiral Byrd's cousin, David Harold "Dry Hole" Byrd.

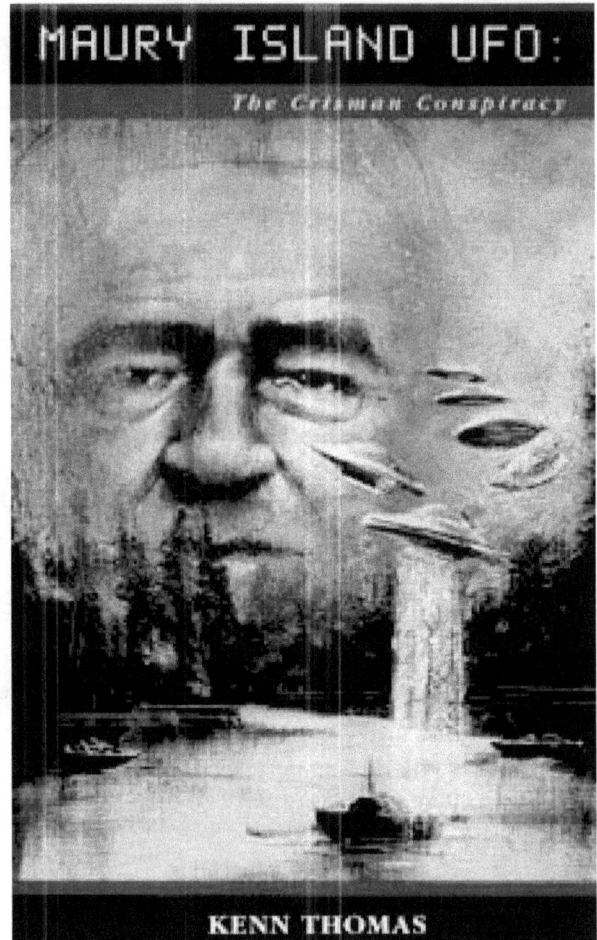

The mysterious Fred Crisman was first associated with the Shaver Mystery, then the UFO crash near Maury Island and ultimately the JFK assassination, as best depicted on cover of book by Kenn Thomas.

Thomas Beckham mugshot photo, New Orleans 6/14/1962

German Nazi Antarctica letter from Buechner/Bernhart book. Suspicious?

A translation of the alleged Nazi Antarctic letter from one of the Buechner/Bernhart books.

Kennedy UFO Memo

07/98   10:03 FAX   ☒004

UNCLASSIFIED 32   THE WHITE HOUSE
                        WASHINGTON

~~CONFIDENTIAL~~   November 12, 1963

NATIONAL SECURITY ACTION MEMORANDUM NO. 271

MEMORANDUM FOR

    The Administrator, National Aeronautics and Space
    Administration

SUBJECT: Cooperation with the USSR on Outer Space Matters

I would like you to assume personally the initiative and central
responsibility within the Government for the development of a
program of substantive cooperation with the Soviet Union in the
field of outer space, including the development of specific technical proposals. I assume that you will work closely with the
Department of State and other agencies as appropriate.

These proposals should be developed with a view to their possible discussion with the Soviet Union as a direct outcome of
my September 20 proposal for broader cooperation between
the United States and the USSR in outer space, including cooperation in lunar landing programs. All proposals or sug-
gestions originating within the Government relating to this
general subject will be referred to you for your consideration
and evaluation.

In addition to developing substantive proposals, I expect that
you will assist the Secretary of State in exploring problems of
procedure and timing connected with holding discussions with
the Soviet Union and in proposing for my consideration the
channels which would be most desirable from our point of
view. In this connection the channel of contact developed

UNCLASSIFIED
~~CONFIDENTIAL~~

Russia ooo.91 (12Nov63)

SecDef Control No. X7448

Kennedy UFO Memo

TOP SECRET

November 12, 1963

MEMORANDUM FOR
The Director, Central Intelligence Agency

SUBJECT: Classification review of all UFO intelligence files affecting
National Security

As I had discussed with you previously, I have initiated [redacted] and
have instructed James Webb to develop a program with the Soviet Union in
joint space and lunar exploration. It would be very helpful if you would have
the high threat cases reviewed with the purpose of identification of bona fide
as opposed to classified CIA and USAF sources. It is important that we
make a clear distinction between the knowns and unknowns in the event the
Soviets try to mistake our extended cooperation as a cover for intelligence
gathering of their defence and space programs.

When this data has been sorted out, I would like you to arrange a program
of data sharing with NASA where Unknowns are a factor. This will help NASA
mission directors in their defensive responsibilities.

I would like an interim report on the data review no later than February 1,
1964.

/S/ John F. Kennedy

Thomas Beckham,
a mysterious preacher.

Thomes Beckham as the mysterious
Mark Evans.

SECRET EXPLOITS OF ADMIRAL RICHARD E. BYRD

REVEALED!

The Underground World of Supermen Discovered by Admiral Byrd . . . Under the North Pole . . . and Kept Secret by U. S. Government

Dr. Raymond Bernard, A.B., M.A., Ph.D., noted scholar and author of "THE HOLLOW EARTH," says that the true home of the flying saucers is a huge underground world whose entrance is at the North Polar opening. Dr. Raymond Bernard believes in the hollow interior of the Earth lives a super race which wants nothing to do with man on the surface. They launched their flying saucers only after man threatened the world with A-Bombs.

Admiral Byrd, says sources quoted by Dr. Bernard, led a Navy team into the polar opening and came upon this underground region. It is free of ice and snow, has mountains covered with forests; lakes, rivers, vegetation and strange animals. But the news of his discovery was suppressed by the U.S. government in order to prevent other nations from exploring the inner world and claiming it.

Now Dr. Bernard in his book "The Hollow Earth" leads you through this subterranean world to meet the civilization which occupies an underground area larger than North America! Beneath the 800 mile crust of the Earth is the greatest discovery in human history inhabited by millions of super intelligent beings. If you are ready for information that not many people can handle, order this book today. Fill out the coupon and send $3.50 for the Soft Bound Edition. Books sold on 10 Day Money Back Guarantee. Limited Edition, Order Now! ▶

CAN YOU EXPLAIN THE FOLLOWING?

- Why does one find tropical seeds, plants and trees floating in the fresh water of icebergs?
- Why do millions of tropical birds and animals go farther North in the wintertime?
- If it is not hollow and warm inside the Earth at the Poles, then why does colored pollen color the Earth for thousands of miles?
- Why is it warmer at the Poles than 600 to 1000 miles away from them?
- Why does the North Wind in the Arctic get warmer as one sails North beyond 70° latitude?

Fielderest Pub. Co., Inc., Dept. PM10
210 5th Ave., New York 10, N.Y.
Please send me "The Hollow Earth" by Dr. Bernard.
☐ I enclose $3.50. Ship postpaid soft cover edition.
☐ I enclose $4.95. Ship postpaid library edition.
NAME...
ADDRESS...
CITY..................... STATE.......... ZIP.........
☐ I enclose $1 deposit. Ship C.O.D. for balance plus postage and handling.

ACT NOW!! DON'T HESITATE!!

This sparkling book will make you wonder and think about the many things that Dr. Raymond Bernard clearly and plainly reveals. The edition is limited, first come first served, money back guarantee.

POPULAR MECHANICS

Widely placed ad for The Hollow Earth, a book by Dr. Raymond Bernard.

SECRET EXPLOITS OF ADMIRAL RICHARD E. BYRD

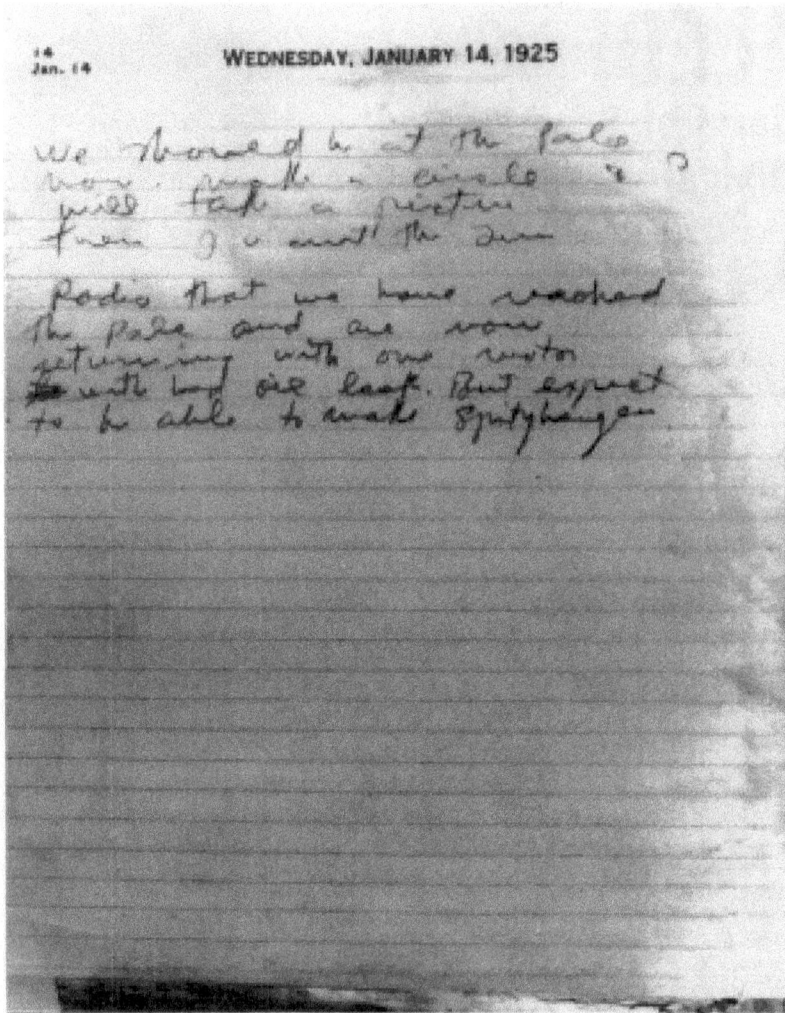

A page from Byrd's lost 1926 diary from his North Pole flights.

FIGURE 2.   Message in Byrd's diary from Byrd to pilot Floyd Bennett, May 9, 1926. Byrd used blank pages from a 1925 diary to make this note. (Courtesy of Ohio State University Archives/Byrd Polar Research Program.)

Seldom pictured logo produced for the 1938/39 Nazi Antarctic expedition.

Photo of David Harold Byrd's Little America Antarctic base replica as seen at the 1936 Texas Centennial Exposition in Dallas.

SECRET EXPLOITS OF ADMIRAL RICHARD E. BYRD

SECRET SOCIETIES AND INFORMATION CONTROL

Richard Byrd was a Freemason, having joined a Washington, D.C., lodge in 1921. It seems being members of secret societies – and the Freemasons, in particular – was a "thing" for explorers of the day. Early, ill-fated Antarctic explorers Scott and Shackleton had been Masons. Author Nicholas Johnson reports in his book "*Cold Dead Place*" that there is still a strong Masonic presence at the Antarctic base.

The mainly volunteer crew at Little America, the base camp for Byrd's 1928 Antarctic expedition, were so unruly that Byrd formed a secret society within the group. Eleven of the 42 men at the base were Masons like Byrd. Byrd's secret society, which he called the Loyal Legion, was obviously based on the Masonic systems of initiation and confidentiality.

In an interview, author and Byrd biographer Eugene Rogers spoke of his discovery of a Loyal Legion document, which he described as one "of the most fantastic things" he found while researching Byrd's first Antarctic exploration.

Rogers stated that Byrd "...got several of the lesser-ranking men on the expedition, the younger men, and actually put them through a secret ceremony in which he read to them the purpose of the Loyal Legion, which was to protect Byrd against mutiny in Antarctica and to protect Byrd's reputation even when they got back to the United States. Byrd made them swear an oath of loyalty to him."

THE FIRST RULE OF LOYAL LEGION IS . . .

The oaths that the initiate had to swear to started with "I will divulge to no one in any way and in any manner anything whatever in connection with the Loyal Legion."

They further had to swear that they would not try and learn the names of other members of the group and, most importantly, that they would do anything that Byrd asked them to do and would not tell anyone that Byrd asked them to do it.

If Byrd needed people around him that were loyal and able to keep secrets, and he found Freemasonry to be a system that facilitated this, his future actions were congruous. On his next Antarctic expedition, which took place in 1934-35, 60 of the 82 members were Freemasons. He established the First Antarctic Lodge No. 777 in February of 1935.

Byrd's third Antarctic expedition was during 1939-40. This would be his first Antarctic expedition with the complete backing of the U.S. government. Coincidently, or perhaps not, this government-sponsored intrusion into the Antarctic happened when the world was at the edge of war.

After World War II, Byrd returned to Antarctica as part of Operation Highjump, which took place in 1946-47. His previous Antarctic mission had government sponsorship; this one was more like a military mission, with Byrd as a figurehead.

Historian David Burk said Highjump was the "most massive military force ever sent to Antarctica," which included well over 4,600 troops, six helicopters, landing-assault vehicles, 13 ships – one being a submarine, another an aircraft carrier – and 23 aircraft.

Along with the stories of Byrd's alleged journey to the Earth's interior, there arose rumors of a secret or missing journal describing his subterranean adventure.

In the early 1980s, a group calling themselves the International Society for a Complete Earth claimed to have obtained a copy of the fabled diary, which they offered for sale. Those who purchased the alleged document were more than likely disappointed. The "diary," which sold for a high price, was more of a pamphlet, and one with lots of space between paragraphs. It was photocopied rather than printed. On top of this, the text was not believable, and few thought it to be genuine. Dennis Crenshaw, publisher of a Hollow Earth magazine, was able to show that some of the words were likely lifted from the 1937 movie "*Lost Horizon*."

Another clue that the diary was likely fake was that it had a short introduction by someone calling himself "Dr. William Bernard." This is very close to the pseudonym "Raymond Bernard" which was used for *The Hollow Earth*, the most widely-known Hollow Earth book – and the book that did the most to circulate the Byrd "beyond the poles" stories.

The October 31, 1978, issue of the *Chicago Tribune* published an interview with the public face of the group, a man with the unlikely name Tawani Shoush. Shoush told how he had a copy of the diary and how his group planned an expedition to the Hollow Earth via the same Antarctic entrance that Byrd had found.

The interviewer felt the need to interrupt the article to note that "...Shoush has a seemingly inordinate fascination with the idea of a 'tall, blond, blue-eyed super race' and with Germany."

People who corresponded with Shoush in the 1980s would note that his spelling and grammatical style seemed German. The logo on his letterhead was a silhouette of a U-boat, suggesting that he was not only German but may have been an actual Nazi.

But this could not be so. Tawani Wakawa Shoush was a Native American. In a 1968 article in which he describes his grandfather's encounter with Bigfoot at Mt. Shasta(!), he says he is of the Modoc tribe.

And his politics seem to have been far to the left. An ad in the July 9th, 1969, *Free Venice Beachhead* (Venice, CA) said that "Red Power leader Nawana (sic) Tawani Shoush" is a contributor to the August 1969 issue of *WIN* – seemingly a New-York-based "hippy" newspaper – along with Allen Ginsburg and Discordian founder Kerry Thornley.

It appears Shoush was red not only in ethnicity but also in politics. His name appears in the archives of more than one communist activist, so it seems that Shoush was a left-wing Native American pretending to be a right-wing German, which doesn't make a lot of sense.

AND THEN IT GETS WEIRD

In the late 1980s and early 1990s, a series of self-published books, dealing with Nazi esoteric history, began to appear on the shelves of counterculture bookstores. Authored by Dr. Howard A. Buechner, they were *"Hitler's Ashes - Seeds of A New Reich," "Adolph Hitler and the Secrets of the Holy Lance,"* and *"Emerald Cup, Ark of Gold: Quest of SS Lieutenant Otto Rahn."*

These Indiana-Jones-esque tales of Nazi relic hunting and hoarding are presented as nonfiction. Two of them, *"Hitler's Ashes"* and *"Secrets of the Holy Lance,"* have an interesting co-author and source – "Capt. Wilhelm Bernhart" – alleged to be a former German U-boat commander. Sound familiar?

"Bernhart" tells a tale of hiding holy relics in Antarctica just before the end of World War II, as well as the discovery of a hole that led deep under the Antarctic surface – albeit one much smaller than in classic "hole at the pole" stories.

He further tells of an expedition, referred to as "The Hartmann Expedition," that successfully recovered the artifacts in 1979.

In the *Chicago Tribune* article, published at the end of 1978, Shoush says that they were planning the expedition to Antarctica in the near future. People who corresponded with Shoush in the 1980s were told that the Antarctic expedition had been successful, and, most incredibly, that they had made contact with the Inner Earth inhabitants.

It appears that Shoush may very well have been a "front" for the pseudonymous Bernard/Bernhart. At one point the website for the International Society for a Complete Earth gave yet another pseudonym for Bernard/Bernhart – "Captain Ritter von X" – and pretty much acknowledged that "Ritter" was behind the ISCE and the Buechner books.

One could make a case that Bernard/Bernhart/Ritter pulled a fast one on Shoush, but Buechner seemed harder to fool. A highly educated medical doctor, Buechner served in World War II and participated in the liberation of the Dachau concentration camp. He wrote about his experience in his book *"Dachau: The Hour of the Avenger."*

Upon Buechner's death in 2003, at the age of 84, his obituary listed his numerous accolades and accomplishments, including having authored 120 medical articles and book chapters.

Around the same time that Shoush was active distributing the questionable Byrd diary, another publisher was busy mixing flying saucer and Hollow-Earth tales with extreme right-wing views. Ernst Zundel, a German immigrant living in

SECRET EXPLOITS OF ADMIRAL RICHARD E. BYRD

Toronto, Canada, had re-written a German book and published it as *"UFOs: Nazi Secret Weapon?"* If one had any doubts as to Zundell's sympathies, you only had to take a look at the titles of his other publications, one of which was *"The Hitler We Loved and Why."*

Despite Zundel's political alliance, his Nazi UFO book was well made, very interesting and proved popular. He promised it was to be part of a series. The second volume was *"Secret Nazi Polar Expeditions."*

In this one, his sympathies were less hidden, but it was to become one of the few sources of information on the exploration of Antarctica by the Nazi government before the outbreak of World War II.

Even less known than the pre-war Nazi polar expeditions is that Byrd had met with the German government. After his second Antarctic expedition, he traveled to Hamburg and was invited to be part of the 1938/39 mission to explore "Neuschwabenland," which he declined. This means that when World War II broke out, an event that pushed Byrd back into military service, he was well aware that the Nazis were intruding into Antarctica, something he could not have been pleased with.

The next volume of Zundel's UFO/Antarctic series was to be titled *"The Last Battalion."* It was to be Zundell's version of Operation Highjump, which he maintained was the last, and secret, battle of World War II. The Nazis had set up a secret base in the Antarctic, he said, and had fought off the U.S. military, out of view of the rest of the world.

This book never got published, as some of Zundel's other publications had gotten him in trouble, and he spent the next few decades in courtrooms fighting one legal battle or another. He self-admittedly was more interested in promoting his controversial political views, with subjects like UFOs being just another way to get them out in the open.

And if the suggestion that there was a secret Nazi base in Antarctica seems farfetched, it's a fact that Byrd's Antarctic expeditions had discovered areas that were naturally heated by geothermal means – and that the Nazis could have found similar areas. Couple this with the fact that many powerful Nazis did escape to South America, including those as notorious as Klaus Barbie and Josef Mengele, and the idea has a disturbing possibility of reality.

But there was something strange about Operation Highjump. The sudden and massive military interest in Antarctica had to have a cause. According to historian David Burke, one of its covert goals, only admitted to years later, was "consolidating and extending U.S. sovereignty over the largest practical area of the continent."

And Byrd did seem to be worried about someone invading via Antarctica. After an interview with Byrd by the International News Service, the March 5, 1947, edition of the Chilean newspaper *El Mercurio* reported "Admiral Richard E. Byrd warned today that the United States should adopt measures of protection against the possibility of an invasion of the country by hostile planes coming from the Polar Regions. The admiral explained that he was not trying to scare anyone, but the cruel reality is that, in case of a new war, the United States could be attacked by planes flying over one or both poles. This statement was made as part of a recapitulation of his own polar experience..."

After Highjump, Byrd participated in one final Antarctic mission, this one also a military operation.

Operation Deep Freeze (1957-58) established permanent bases in Antarctica. It was coordinated with the International Geological Year, which was a multi-country scientific effort to learn more about the true nature of the planet. Byrd was only a part of Deep Freeze for one week. He returned to the United States on February 3, 1956, and would never return to the Polar Regions. He died a little over a year later, in March of 1957, at his home in Boston.

MISSING PAPERS AND SECRET DIARIES

And what about the tales of secret or missing journals and papers? Could there be any truth to this, or is it all jumbled misinformation or disinformation?

There is plenty of reason to believe that Byrd and others suppressed information about his polar mission.

As previously noted, Byrd had a desire to control information coming out about his missions and he used the systemized secrecy of the Masons and his own quasi-Masonic Loyal Legion to control his crew.

But it went beyond this. Byrd allowed journalists on his first Antarctic expedition, but no story was to be released without his approval. He censored radio messages and made his crew turn over their photos and negatives so he would be the only person that the media could ask for information about the expedition.

Later, it was not just Byrd controlling the information, but the government as well. On the second Antarctic mission, President Roosevelt ordered "the surrender of all journals, diaries, memorabilia, remarks, writings, charts, drawings, sketches, paintings, photographs, films, plates, as well as specimens of any kind." And with Highjump, the military had taken over, with its own institutionalized methodology of secrecy.

And there is at least one missing diary, and we know who made it go missing. The Hearst papers offered crew member Smith $15,000 for a story on the first Antarctic expedition. Smith discovered that his diary had been stolen from his locker. Byrd ordered the ship searched, saying he had no idea who took the diary. Later, a crew member – presumably a disloyal member of the Loyal Legion – confessed that he had taken the diary on Byrd's orders.

After Byrd's death, his family allowed no access to his papers, and, because of this, Byrd biographies were based on sanitized, public information.

Per the *Boston Globe* of February 1, 1987, "Because of disagreements within Byrd's family over the final disposition of the estate, for nearly 30 years his papers gathered dust or moldered in the scattered attics, warehouses, bank vaults, and basements where they had been stored. Over the decades many documents were lost or mislaid, others were damaged by dampness or mishandling."

In 1985, Byrd's family gave his papers to Ohio State University, but it was not until 1993 that they could get funding to sort and catalogue the collection. In 1996, they found a lost Byrd diary. It was an account of his controversial 1926 north polar flight, found in a box that was supposed to contain artifacts, not papers, and mislabeled "1925."

It has no account of the fabled Inner Earth journey, and the entries only added to the controversy as to whether he had reached the pole. The journal was so informal in style and the entries so haphazard that it made the entries in the Society for Complete Earth's Byrd diary seem more reasonable.

That the diary was found at all was only luck. As previously noted, there could be many papers that were simply lost or destroyed before they were placed in the archive.

Journals or papers that Byrd (or someone else) didn't want the world to see would have been completely removed, if any existed. The Highjump expedition was the most likely to have interesting findings, the most subject to military control, and also one of the least documented in the Byrd archives, according to the Ohio State University webpage.

A TRAGIC FOOTNOTE

Admiral Byrd's son, Richard Jr., who was said to be "completely devoted to keeping alive the memory of his father," had been head of the Admiral Byrd Foundation. The foundation had been started by Byrd's widow, and it controlled the Byrd papers and artifacts. It was in 1984, immediately before the Ohio State University acquisition, that the building which housed the Byrd records changed ownership and many became lost.

In September 1988, Richard Byrd, Jr., was scheduled to appear at an event at the Washington, D.C. National Geographic Society headquarters honoring his father. He left on a train for Washington but he never made it to the event. Three weeks later, his body was found in an abandoned Baltimore warehouse. The cause of death was dehydration and malnutrition.

A STRANGE CONNECTION TO THE JOHN F. KENNEDY ASSASSINATION

Byrd's cousin, David Harold Byrd, was instrumental in funding Byrd's polar expeditions before the government took over. Harold Byrd promoted the expeditions quite literally like carnival attractions, having a replica of the Antarctic base Little America set up at the 1936 Texas Centennial Exposition. Richard Byrd showed his appreciation by naming an Antarctic mountain range after his cousin and bene-factor.

Harold Byrd's oil wealth granted him entry into the inner circle of Texas power. He was a member of the 8F Group, an elite organization named after the room number of the Lamar Hotel in Houston where they held meetings. The group of predominately right-wing businessmen had Lyndon Johnson and John Connelly in its ranks. 8F also coordinated political activities with other Southern right-wing politicians and businessmen, including Billie Sol Estes and Clint Murchison. These are names that are very familiar to researchers who have investigated Lyndon Johnson's connections to the JFK assassination.

Byrd also employed Mac Wallace, a man who some think was Lyndon Johnson's personal hit man – with some even going so far as to suggest Wallace fired the shots that came from the sixth-floor window of the Texas School Book Depository. Wallace worked for Harold Byrd's aviation company TEMCO, which handled defense contracts and required a security clearance for its employees. The problem was that Wallace had previously been convicted of capi-tal murder, so someone must have pulled some strings to enable his employment – most likely Lyndon Johnson.

And if those connections weren't enough, Harold Byrd likely knew JFK-as-sassination figures George de Morenschildt, David Atlee Philips, and George H. W. Bush through their mutual membership in the Dallas Petroleum Club.

George de Morenschildt was an interesting individual, to say the least. At various times in his life, he was connected to Nazis and the CIA. In addition to being a member of the aforementioned Dallas Petroleum Club, he and Harold Byrd were mutual members of Texas Crusade for Freedom, The Dallas Council On World Affairs, and The Crusade For A Free Europe. All of these were right-wing groups, and the last two were almost certainly CIA connected.

De Morenschildt had another friend: Lee Harvey Oswald. Oswald was an odd choice for a de Morenschildt associate – Oswald supposedly being a pro-communist American who defected to Russia and de Morenschildt being a right-wing White Russian who once was part of a pro-Nazi plot to assassinate Stalin. Researchers suspect that de Morenschildt was one of Oswald's "handlers." De Morenschildt was being investigated by the House Select Committee on Assassi-nations in regard to his connections to Oswald but committed suicide before he could be interviewed.

David Atlee Philips was deeply involved in the framing of Oswald in New Orleans, Mexico City, and Dallas. House Select Committee investigator Gaeton Fonzi was convinced that Philips was also "Maurice Bishop," a pseudonym for a CIA agent who was high up in anti-Cuban operations. Antonio Veciana, founder of the anti-Castro group Alpha 66, had seen "Bishop" and Oswald together in Dallas shortly before the assassination. It was not until years later that Veciana confirmed that "Bishop" and Philips were one and the same.

Byrd also, in 1941, founded the Civil Air Patrol. As most JFK-assassination researchers know, Lee Harvey Oswald met David Ferrie in the CAP. The eccentric David Ferrie became the focus of New Orleans district attorney Jim Garrison's investigation into the JFK-assassination plot but died under strange circumstances before he could be brought to trial. There is a strong possibility that Byrd knew Ferrie.

Harold Byrd owned the Texas School Book Depository, the building that Oswald worked at, and the alleged location of the fatal shots. Byrd bought the building in 1939. There has been much speculation as to how Oswald ended up on the route of the presidential motorcade. He seemed to have been manipulated in the months preceding the assassination. George de Morenschildt had introduced the Oswalds to Ruth and Michael Paine, a couple who were outwardly Quakers but had family connections that tied them to intelligence agencies. They provided Oswald with job leads. Oswald almost got a job with Trans Texas Airways, which would have put him at Love Field Airport, where Kennedy arrived in Dallas that day.

Harold Byrd was not in Dallas the day Kennedy was shot. He was on safari in Africa with his friend General Jim Doolittle. Researcher Richard Bartholomew wrote, "Byrd prepared well for the trip: Temco, Inc. was an aircraft company founded by D.H. Byrd and which later merged with his friend James Ling's electronics company (1960), and aircraft manufacturer Chance Vought Corporation (1961) to form Ling-Temco-Vought (LTV). Byrd became a director of LTV and bought, along with Ling, 132,000 shares of LTV in November 1963. Byrd then left the country to go on his two-month safari in central Africa. He returned in January to find his good friend Lyndon Johnson president of the United States, his building famous, and a large defense contract awarded to LTV to build fighter planes – to be paid for out of the 1965 budget which had not yet been approved by Congress."

When Byrd returned from Africa, he had the window that Oswald allegedly fired from – the window of the sniper's nest – removed and kept it as a souvenir. He morbidly decorated the bottom half of the window with newspaper clippings of the assassination and postcard pictures of Kennedy, Dealey Plaza, and his Book Depository. He framed it and put it in the banquet room of his mansion, where it remained until the day he died in 1986.

UFO CONNECTIONS TO THE JFK ASSASSINATION

There are numerous strange connections between the JFK assassination and UFOs. Perhaps the best known involves Fred Lee Crisman.

Crisman was subpoenaed by New Orleans district attorney Jim Garrison as

Q. Have you ever had occasion to make a phone call to Van Nuys, California?

A. Oh yes, on several occasions.

Q. Who were you calling in Van Nuys, California?

A. I say several occasions, I shouldn't say it that way; Dr. Frank E Stranges.

Q. Anybody else in Van Nuys?

A. Pardon?

Q. Did you ever call anybody else in Van Nuys?

A. Nobody.

Q. What kind of doctor is Frank E. Stranges?

A. Dr. Frank E. Stranges is a member of the National Investigation Committee on Unidentified Flying Objects, he is also the author of several books, he owns a DPS, which is a Doctor of Psychology

Jim Garrison asks Thomas Beckham about Frank Stranges

part of his JFK-assassination investigation. Garrison accused him of being a CIA agent. Some have suggested that he was the actual gunman. A photo analysis by the House Select Committee on Assassinations suggested that he was one of the three tramps arrested behind the grassy knoll.

Crisman was already known to UFO investigators for his part in the Maury Island Incident, an early UFO case that turned tragic when two Air Force investigators carrying alleged flying-saucer debris died in a plane crash.

Ray Palmer, publisher of *"Flying Saucers"* magazine – the very same magazine that would publish the accounts of Byrd's journeys into the Inner Earth – had sent flying-saucer witness Kenneth Arnold to document the Maury Island sighting. Arnold was there for the investigation, including the death of the Air Force men. The result was one of the first UFO books, *"The Coming of the Saucers."*

Researchers discovered another link between Crisman and Palmer. Not long before the Maury Island Incident, when Palmer was editor of *"Amazing Stories"* and promoting the Shaver Mystery, Crisman had written a letter describing his encounter with underground beings. He wrote that during World War II, he had been trapped in a cave in Burma that was filled with Dero, Shaver's name for evil underground dwellers.

He and a companion, Crisman's letter said, fought their way out with machine guns, but not without sustaining an injury from one of the Dero beam-weapons.

Crisman and his friend, Thomas Beckham, who was also a subject of Garrison's investigation, were into all kinds of strange things. At one point, Beckham had connections to employees of the Guy Banister detective agency, which likely was involved with Lee Harvey Oswald. Beckham, using the stage name Mark Evans, was pursuing a country music career with Crisman as his manager. At the same time, Crisman was the host of a right-wing radio show under the pseudonym Jon Gold.

Crisman and Beckham were quite a team. Together they cooked up correspondence courses and diploma-mill schemes, and the duo also organized flying saucer and paranormal clubs and meetings.

Frank Stranges, a man who truly lived up to his name, was a part of the Crisman-and-Beckham orbit. Stranges was an evangelist who claimed to have met a man from Venus at the Pentagon. He claimed to hold many degrees, including one in criminology from one of Crisman and Beckham's correspondence courses.

Stranges was often a speaker at Crisman and Beckham's flying-saucer clubs. Jim Garrison took a slight interest in Stranges, enough to ask Beckham who Stranges was during their grand jury depositions. Garrison's interest in Stranges likely stemmed from the fact that several of the suspects in his investigation had membership in religious organizations of questionable derivation, which he believed may have been a cover for intelligence organizations.

Frank Stranges was also a Hollow Earth believer, or at least presented himself as one. He offered audio tapes of his lectures, "*The Hollow Earth Theory Explored*" and "*Your Paradise Inside This Planet,*" as well as a book, "*Nazi UFO Secrets and Bases Exposed.*"

Although some would dismiss Crisman and Beckham as cranks and conmen, both had connections that are difficult to deny. In addition to Beckham's connections to the Banister detective agency, there is film footage that seems to show Beckham with Oswald.

Crisman had a history with the military, worked for Boeing, had right-wing political connections – even to the infamous Minute Men – and was obviously hyper-intelligent.

In the 1960s, the FBI and the CIA were using political fringe groups and individuals to do things that they legally could not. People with borderline criminal personalities, like so many of Garrison's suspects, would be just the kind of people that would be recruited for illegal domestic operations.

SECRET EXPLOITS OF ADMIRAL RICHARD E. BYRD

Richard E. Byrd

Sponsored by the Masonic Stamp Club of N.Y.

WASHINGTON, D.C.
SEP 14
1988
20066

FIRST DAY OF ISSUE

USA 25
Richard E. Byrd

Richard Evelyn Byrd 1888-1957
Initiated, Passed and Raised 1921
Federal Lodge No. 1, Washington D.C.
Affiliated Kane Lodge No. 454, N.Y.C., 1928
Distinguished Achievement Medal
Grand Lodge of New York, May 4, 1947

Colorano "Silk" First Day Cover

First Day Cover issued by the U.S. Post Office depicts Masonic symbol next to Admiral Byrd's portrait.

The connections to UFOs and the JFK assassination go beyond Garrison's investigation. Warren Commission member Gerald Ford had a UFO connection. In 1966 Ford was a Michigan congressman and Minority Leader of the House of Representatives. After a series of UFO sightings in his state, which the Air Force infamously dismissed as "swamp gas," a seemingly outraged Ford publicly called for a Congressional investigation into UFOs. Surprisingly, this happened later that year, which in turn led to the creation of a supposedly independent study of UFOs by the University of Colorado.

Later it became clear that the report's conclusions had been predetermined – much like the Warren Report – and that the whole point had been to create a way to close the Air Force's public UFO investigation. Ford never openly looked into UFOs again, even when he became president and would presumably have more influence and access.

Another odd UFO/JFK-assassination connection is Col. Philip Corso. Corso is best known for his controversial book "*The Day After Roswell*," in which he claimed to have been involved in a project that back-engineered technology from a crashed flying saucer. Less known is that, near the end of his life, he was working on a book to be titled "*The Day After Dallas*." Corso had been a Senate Investigator for Warren Commission member Senator Richard Russell, who was one of its few dissenting members. "*The Day After Dallas*" was to be an account of an investigation of the Warren Commission itself, and it may see publication in the future, after the people it could embarrass have passed on.

There are many more connections between UFOs and the assassination, enough that even a semi-complete listing would take several pages. Over the years there have been rumors that the reason JFK was assassinated was because he was going to make a public revelation about the true nature of UFOs.

Two documents have emerged, letters from Kennedy to the CIA and NASA, which give some credibility to this allegation.

The letters, obtained by author William Lester under the Freedom of Information Act, talk of plans for a shared USA/Russian space program and requests the release of UFO information for the purpose of sharing it with the Russians.

The CIA memo, dated November 12, 1963, states: "It would be very helpful if you would have the high threat cases reviewed with the purpose of identification of bona fide as opposed to classified CIA and USAF sources. It is important that we make a clear distinction between the knowns and unknowns in the event the Soviets try to mistake our extended cooperation as a cover for intelligence gathering of their defense and space programs. I would like you to arrange a program of data sharing with NASA where unknowns are a factor."

The NASA memo, dated the same day as the CIA memo, called for "cooperation with the former Soviet Union on mutual outer space activities," including lunar landings.

JFK was assassinated just ten days later. Instead of Kennedy's desired cooperative space effort, the race to the moon was used to heat up the Cold War even further. Instead of UFO revelations, the path was laid to shut down UFO information.

05

A TREATISE CONCERNING THE
HITLER-UFO-SATANIC CONNECTION
A NOTE FROM CONTRIBUTOR TIM CRIDLAND

The following essay originally appeared in my 'zine "Off The Deep End." The author – or authors – seemed to be part of some kind of art collective that also produced industrial music.

I cautioned the reader in taking this at face value. The industrial music scene incorporated various aspects of art movements like Dada and surrealism, including the concept of "aesthetic terrorism."

The essay may have been intended to create the idea of a strange Nazi-esque occult group rather than actually being one. In other words, it may be less Alt-Right and more Alt-That's-Just-Wrong.

Whatever the case, the people who wrote this essay do seem to be well versed in esoteric Nazi lore and the occult traditions in general. As with anything of this nature, the statements made should be thoroughly researched before being repeated as fact. Caveat Emptor.

* * * * *

(This article was penned by persons who wish to be known only as "The Final Solution" and was originally published in the 1980s. It is a nakedly pro-Hitler take on the subject of the Hollow Earth and the creatures said to live down there, and we present it only for its historical interest and relevance to the topic of our book. We are not sympathetic to the Nazi philosophy in any way, and the reader is hereby warned about this section's "warm and fuzzy" affection for Hitler.)

The first light that touched the infant Hitler's soft pink skin also touched the town of Bramau-am-inn, near the Austrian border. At that time, Bramau-am-inn was known as the birthplace of both mediums and mystics; thus the seed of occult knowledge was already inside the babe Hitler. When Adolph Hitler first beheld the so-called "Spear of Destiny" he experienced a vision which he could not speak of . . .

In the early days of the war, Hitler, a man capable of intense anxiety and nervousness, was quite calm in his conquests of Europe. He acted in power because he knew through occult vision that he would meet no resistance, we are told. But where did he get these strange powers? The seed did not sprout by itself. There was help from occult gardeners. He was assisted by such secret societies as the Golden Dawn, the Vril Society and the Thule Society.

The Golden Dawn was formed in the United Kingdom circa 1885 by S.L. MacGregor Mathers in association with Wynn Westcott and others. Mathers was in contact with a group of "super beings" or "praeter-human intelligences," which held office as the "Secret Chiefs" of the Great White Brotherhood. Mathers described them in a letter to the "members of the Second Order":

"As for me, I believe they are human beings living on this Earth but endowed with terrible supernatural powers."

The rituals of the Golden Dawn were based on papers drawn up by Eliphas Levi in the 19th century, and the order attracted the attention of famous writers, artists and English leaders such as Bram Stoker, W.B. Yeats, Aleister Crowley and Bulwer Lytton. Lytton's book, "The Coming Race," influenced both the Vril Society and Adolf Hitler profoundly. We shall discuss this shortly.

An early member of the Golden Dawn was Karl Haushoffer. He was known as "the General with Second Sight." Rudolph Hess studied geopolitics under Haushoffer's direction. Haushoffer advised the writing of "Mein Kampf" and suggested the swastika as the party symbol. Haushoffer had toured the East, and it was while in Asia that he began investigating the Buddhist tradition of Agharta, the name of the underground world. Mongolian monks are said to be in contact with the "under-people." Perhaps this is the reason that Haushoffer stated, "He who controls Mongolia will control the world."

Of mutual friends between Aleister Crowley and Adolf Hitler, two are most notable: Martha Kuntzel, who translated "Liber Legis" or "The Book of the Law," a manuscript which foretold the coming of "a prophet," Adolf Hitler, into Germany. And Captain J.F.C. Fuller, a student of 666 and reportedly "the only Englishman that Hitler liked." Captain Fuller was the only Briton invited to Adolf's 50th birthday celebration.

Let us now examine Hitler's involvement with the Vril and Thule societies. The Thule was a Germanic Magical Order similar to the Pansophia, founded by Herr Tranker, or the German O.T.O. and those then labeled "the German Rosicrucian Movement." The Vril Society was a philosophical order based on Vril energy. According to H.P. Blavatsky, "We can understand the necessity for concealing from the herd such secrets as the Vril, or the rock-destroying force, discovered by John W. Keely of Philadelphia, Pennsylvania."

It was also Keely, in the 19th century, who discovered "perpetual motion." Elsewhere in "The Secret Doctrine," Blavatsky notes, "If the question is asked why Mr. Keely was not allowed to pass a certain limit, the answer is easy: it is because that which he has unconsciously discovered is the terrible sidereal force, known to and named by the Aryan Rishis in their Astra Vidya by a name we do not like to give."

Hitler became aware of the Vril through Lytton's novel, "The Coming Race," which suggested that a race of highly advanced beings living underground had in its control a force called "Vril-Ya," a power associated with the Hindu Prana, the Cabalistic Yesod, the Telesma of Hermes, Schroedinger's Negative Entropy or the Alchemical Quintessence. As early as 1936, Hitler was sending teams of spelunkers into caves and mines all over Europe, searching for Vril-Ya. The Nazis had also explored Antarctica extensively during the years 1937-38, where they found, like Admiral Byrd, warm water lakes and, as Byrd doubtlessly found, the bigger of the two polar entrances to the Hollow Earth. It is there that they no doubt had a summit with the "ubermen" or supermen at the Gates of Eden itself, in the legendary polar rim city, "Rainbow City."

Hitler was quoted as having said of these "extraterrestrials": "The New Man is living amongst us now; he is here. Isn't that enough for you? I will tell you a secret: I have seen the New Man. He is intrepid and cruel. I was afraid of Him."

While the Vril Society's official view was that, "The world will change. The Lords will emerge from the center of the Earth. Unless we have made an alliance with them and become Lords ourselves, we shall find ourselves among the slaves on the dung-heap that will feed the roots of the new cities that will arise."

Tim Cridland

©Tim Cridland 2016

Journey to the center of the Earth

06

THE PARANORMAL TOURIST:
Q AND A WITH TIM SWARTZ
By Sean Casteel

Tim Swartz's interest in UFOs began in his childhood, but not in the way you might expect. Way back in 1968, his third grade class was told to give reports on current events, and   Swartz was assigned an article on a UFO flap that was ongoing at the time.

"I didn't know anything about UFOs," he recalled, "and didn't really care about UFOs. But I gave my report and was just instantly pegged for the rest of my life by my fellow students as 'the Flying Saucer Guy.' I was the guy who believed in little green men and Martians. Even though I didn't know a flying saucer from Adam. But that was the role I was given."

But the interesting part was still to come. Some of the same people who laughed at Swartz when others were around would later approach him and quietly talk about their own UFO and ghost experiences. It became a familiar pattern for Swartz.

"They wanted somebody to listen to their story," he said, "and basically just tell them they're not crazy. Then they go off and you can tell that a huge weight has been lifted."

The fact that so many people were telling surprisingly similar stories brought it home to Swartz that something must really be going on. He would end up, of course, dedicating a large portion of his life to the subject.

I knew going in that Swartz has a history of traveling the world seeking the answers to various paranormal mysteries. When I asked him about exactly where he had gone, he laughed and said "I've been everywhere, man."

It all began in the 1980s, when Swartz worked as a videographer and producer for a PBS station in Indianapolis, Indiana, their local Channel 20, which was the flagship station at the time for all the other PBS stations in the state. The station had a for-profit arm that would hire out their film crews to other production companies, which led to Swartz working for all the major networks in the U.S. and even some foreign networks. Swartz also worked as an official videographer for the State of Indiana, specifically for then-governor Evan Bayh.

While working for a Channel 20 syndicated program called "The Morning Ag Report," Swartz was tapped to be part of the overseas film crew that accompanied state and federal agriculture officials on fact-finding trips far and wide. The list of countries Swartz visited is long, and includes England, Germany, Poland, Bulgaria, Turkey, Russia, Hong Kong, China, Japan, South Korea, Egypt and Nairobi.

In preparation for many of those overseas assignments, Swartz would set up meetings with local researchers and experts involved with UFOs and other types of paranormal investigation.

"For example, in Egypt," Swartz said, "I met with somebody from Cairo who was familiar with a lot of tunnels and other things that government officials don't talk about. And they don't like it being broadcast to the tourists that these things are there. We got to examine some of these unique places on the Giza Plateau that not everybody gets a chance to see."

In the early 1990s, Swartz made the acquaintance of another Tim, Timothy Green Beckley, and began to write articles for Beckley's "UFO Universe Magazine" as well as writing numerous books for Beckley's publishing house, Global Communications. Swartz also wrote screenplays and did some directing and videography work for Beckley's line of horror movies, with titles like "The Curse of Ed Wood" and "Skin-Eating Jungle Vampires."

The theory of the Hollow Earth was also of great interest to Swartz, and, beginning as a youth, he read voraciously on the subject – like Tarzan creator Edgar Rice Burroughs' "Pellucidar" series of action/adventure books set in a fictional Hollow Earth where prehistoric animals and various tribes of humans dwelt.

"Burroughs obviously did his research," Swartz said. "Because he had the polar openings and how the inner Earth is bathed in perpetual sunlight because the sun that hung in the sky there could never set. It always looked like you were living in the bottom of a giant bowl. There was a telepathic master race that kept everyone else enslaved. Just wonderful adventure books for teenagers."

Meanwhile, in the nonfiction world, Beckley had written "The Shaver Mystery and the Inner Earth" for legendary paranormal publisher Gray Barker, and it was a must-read for Swartz.

The Hollow Earth theory continued to transform and evolve, and Swartz and Beckley's writing kept pace with the changes.

"By the 1990s, you had all kinds of interesting things," Swartz said, "like the idea of secret military underground bases and the possibility that there are aliens underground controlling things. It's amazing how something that originated in the 19th century is still with us today. It's just taken on different personas and become intertwined with the whole UFO mystery."

SECRET EXPLOITS OF ADMIRAL RICHARD E. BYRD

Swartz has become the "resident expert" for Global Communications on Admiral Byrd and the Hollow Earth mystery, having penned such page-turners as "The Secret Lost Diary of Admiral Richard E. Byrd and the Phantom of the Poles" and "Admiral Byrd's Secret Journey Beyond the Poles." What follows is Swartz fielding questions about a subject that has long fascinated him and which likely has come to fascinate you as well.

*   *   *   *

Question: Can you give me some biographical background on Admiral Byrd? What kind of career did he have prior to his going to the South Pole? Why was it deemed appropriate for him to lead the expedition?

Swartz: Well, before he was Admiral Byrd, he was Richard Evelyn Byrd, Jr. and he was born in 1888. He was born right in that time when the Wright Brothers were doing their innovative work with airplanes. Byrd was extremely fascinated by airplanes and he learned to fly fairly early on. He recognized the potential of airplanes – not only for commercial reasons but for military reasons as well. So Byrd was one of the early forerunners to promote the idea of using airplanes for military purposes.

Byrd graduated from the Naval Academy in 1912 and was commissioned an ensign in the U.S. Navy. His first assignment was on the battleship the U.S.S. Wyoming. By the time World War I rolled around, he was technically retired, but Byrd was able to serve as a retired officer on active duty. He volunteered to become a naval aviator. He took flying lessons and earned his pilot's wings in 1917. This was something he had wanted to do for a long, long time.

Byrd had also been interested in exploration. By that time, most of the world had already been pretty much explored. He had been an avid reader since he was young of adventure books, books detailing expeditions to, say, Africa, South America, overseas expeditions. He'd always been fascinated with that. By his time, the only things that were left to explore would be the Polar Regions. Since the early 19th century, there had been explorations of the North and South Pole to try to discover what was there. But Byrd figured that, with his expertise, especially with aircraft, that he would be able to make inroads into further exploration of the Polar Regions.

His first trip was in 1926, when, along with a pilot named Floyd Bennett, he attempted to fly over the North Pole in a tri-motor monoplane. He had been financed by the Ford Motor Company to make this flight. It lasted about fourteen to fifteen hours, and they claimed to have reached the North Pole, covering a distance of about 1,500 miles. They encircled it and then managed to make it back safely. So when he returned to the U.S., he was a national hero. You know, in 1926, this was the Roaring Twenties, when people were eager for new and different things. So the U.S. embraced Byrd as a national hero. Congress even passed a special act that promoted him to the rank of commander, and then they awarded him the National Medal of Honor. From that point on, to the U.S., Byrd could do no wrong, even though, years later, there has been doubt cast on whether or not they actually made this flight over the North Pole as they said they had. It's one of those things that haters are going to hate, I suppose. There's no way to know, other than their word, whether they actually made it as close to the North Pole as possible. I'm going to give them the benefit of the doubt. Naturally, it's easy to criticize somebody after they're dead and gone and they can't defend themselves.

In 1927, Byrd announced he was going to make a transatlantic flight with the backing of private investors. So again, with pilot Floyd Bennett and some other crew members, he was attempting a transatlantic flight. But unfortunately, during one of the test runs, Byrd' airplane crashed and it was Charles Lindberg who actually ended up reaching that particular milestone first in 1927. Then later on, Byrd actually did complete a flight across the Atlantic from June 29 to July 1 in 1927. He was again given great honor in the U.S. when he returned and was awarded the Distinguished Flying Cross by the then-Secretary of the Navy. After that, Byrd's interest turned towards Antarctica. He was involved in the first Antarctic expedition in 1930. This involved two ships and three airplanes. The idea was for it to be a photographic and geological expedition to try to establish whether there was anything in Antarctica mineral-wise that might be useful. Byrd was involved in at least three Antarctic expeditions before Operation High Jump, so he was no stranger to Antarctica. In fact, on his second Antarctic expedition, in 1934, he spent five winter months alone operating a meteorological station. He almost died from carbon monoxide poisoning because the stove he had malfunctioned.

Question: This was around the time when Byrd visited Nazi Germany?

Swartz: Yes, in late 1938, Byrd actually visited Nazi Germany because he was invited to participate in the 1938-1939 German Antarctic expedition. And he was wined and dined. The Germans had been very impressed by Byrd's knowledge and experience regarding Antarctica. But due to the political conditions at the time, Byrd declined. But then the Germans continued not only with that expedition but also a number of others, probably establishing several bases in the region, beginning then and lasting through the duration of World War II.

THE MYSTERIES SURROUNDING OPERATION HIGHJUMP

Question: So now tell me about Operation Highjump.

Swartz: Operation High Jump was first conceived in 1946, shortly after the end of World War II. Secretary of the Navy James Forestall appointed Byrd his officer-in-charge of Antarctic development. Operation High Jump is extremely odd overall. Considering that, at the time, right after the end of World War II, the Navy was decommissioning a lot of ships, putting lots of them in mothballs. There really wasn't any reason to use them anymore. And then suddenly Secretary Forestall said we need to get a lot of these ships back into operation again because we're going to make this "scientific" expedition to Antarctica.

To date, it's been the largest such expedition ever. It was expected to last six to eight months, which is a huge amount of time. This expedition was supported by a huge naval force and commanded by Rear Admiral Richard Cruzen. There were thirteen U.S. Navy support ships, six helicopters, six flying boats, two seaplanes and fifteen other aircraft. Plus probably 4,000 personnel going along for this so-called "scientific" expedition. You have to understand, this was an enormous operation. And that's where the mystery begins. Why would you need such a gargantuan naval force for just an exploratory scientific expedition?

And, of course, anyone can speculate about this in many different ways and they have. But the expedition arrived in December 1946. They made explorations using airplanes of an area about the size of the U.S. They discovered ten new mountain ranges and gathered an amazing amount of information. One really unusual thing about all this is that they arrived in December 1946 and, in about three weeks' time, they decided they were done exploring, even though they were originally supposed to be there around six months.

No real official explanation has ever been given about why they suddenly decided to leave that quickly. In that short time, they did accomplish a lot of things, and if they had stayed longer, what more might they have discovered? Some people have speculated that they went there in search of a secret Nazi base hidden somewhere along the coast of Antarctica. At the end of World War II, there were a number of German U-boats that had left the Canary Islands carrying personnel, equipment, supplies and things like that. They would later surrender in Argentina but without all this personnel and equipment onboard. Now, one of the U-boat captains said that they had dropped off their people, equipment, etc. at a secret base in Antarctica. And declassified documents show that this could be one of the reasons why this expedition Operation High Jump had been established, to find out just what was going on in Antarctica.

SUSPECTED NAZI INVOLVEMENT

You have to realize that at

World traveler, Tim Swartz, investigated strange and bizarre events in many different countries.

SECRET EXPLOITS OF ADMIRAL RICHARD E. BYRD

Assignment: China

< Assignment: Austria

Assignment: Izmir

From the pyramids of Eqypt
to the
streets of Warsaw.

Tim can be seen in several television episodes of "Ancient Aliens."

the time, just after the end of World War II, there were Nazi officials, intelligence officers, scientists, high-ranking officers who had disappeared out of Europe. And speculation had it that they were heading to South America. A lot of them didn't show up in South America, so the U.S. and the Allied Forces wanted to know where they were. One of the big fears was that they had established something like a Fourth Reich command somewhere in Antarctica. So there's a possibility that Operation High Jump had been basically a military operation to ascertain whether this was true or not. And if it was true, then the response was to invade, take it over, or perhaps even conduct a diplomatic mission. Because if this was true, if a lot of high-ranking scientists and Nazi officials had escaped to Antarctica, this would have been gold to get ahold of, especially by the U.S. These were people that would have been highly prized for various reasons. So we have to get these people and get them alive. And we also have to get the possible equipment and secret weaponry that may have been taken out of Europe and hidden away in Antarctica.

So there's a very good possibility with Operation High Jump that this was the real reason that they were there. The speculation over the years has been that one of the reasons they left early was that Operation High Jump had been ambushed by, say, Nazi flying saucers or some kind of secret weaponry and they were driven away. I have not uncovered any decent evidence to show that's true. This expedition had over 4,000 men, and something like that would be very difficult to keep secret. Even though, with the sailors, it's part of their job to agree not to talk. But, as you've seen, especially with the UFO mystery, you have a lot of people who may have been involved in UFO recovery that on their deathbed admitted that, "Yeah, yeah, this was actually true."

But these men associated with Operation High Jump did not mention anything about being attacked or other members of their crew being killed by some kind of Nazi attack or whatever. So there's a good possibility that they went there and didn't find what they were looking for. Or they DID find what they were looking for, but it wasn't as big of an operation or   secret base as they thought it was going to be. Based on the testimony of the German U-boat captain, this was a pretty good-sized base and was being manned by several thousand high-ranking and elite German squadrons. And it was heavily fortified and heavily protected.

You have to understand that Antarctica is not a pleasant place to live, and it's extremely difficult to establish any kind of large operation there. You have to consider the huge amount of fuel that has to be used just to keep warm every day. So unless the Germans had actually discovered an underground cavern system, which is one of the possibilities that has been talked about over the years, and that this cavern system was warmed by, say, volcanic springs, something along those lines, then more than likely this so-called secret base in Antarctica wasn't actually there and the secret Nazi operation at the end of World War II had actually established itself in South America. The whole Antarctica thing may have just been a red herring situation.

Nazi Germany had been interested in Antarctica during World War II because of the possibility that there was some kind of entranceway into the Hollow Earth there. Hitler had sent a number of expeditions around the world, especially to places like Tibet and Nepal and parts of South America, in search of these entranceways into the Hollow Earth because their occult beliefs had it that the Hollow Earth was populated by the Root Race, the Aryan people. Hitler and his cronies believed that the Aryans were the rightful owners of the world and that they originated from some kind of Super Race that lived in some kind of underground super-civilization. And that there were entranceways, especially around the Himalayas, South America and possibly even Antarctica. So a number of expeditions had been sent to these areas to try to find these entranceways, to get down in there and establish contact with their ancestors, basically, is what they believed. And then hopefully to establish diplomatic relations and to get help in winning the war against the rest of us slovenly bunch.

Let me backtrack a little. The story since the 19th century was that there are openings at the North and South Polar Regions and that these openings are large enough that you could walk or fly into them without even realizing that you had done so. Now here in the 21st century, unless there has been really a massive disinformation campaign going on and photographs of the area have been doctored – I'm not saying that that's not possible, but I'm saying that's unlikely – it's probably not true that these mythical polar openings actually exist. Especially in the Arctic regions because it's all ocean there. It would be a little more difficult, I suppose, to have a giant opening into the Hollow Earth.

At Antarctica, on the other hand, there could actually BE an opening into a cavernous world. You have mountains and it's a giant landmass down there. There have been satellite photographs taken that show some kind of opening in Antarctica and some kind of southern polar light is coming out of this giant cavern. It could very well be that one of these Nazi expeditions actually did discover one of these cavern entranceways into a subterranean part of the world. Whether or not they really made contact with underground dwellers – that remains to be seen.

GREEN AND PLEASANT AND VERY STRANGE

Question: What about Admiral Byrd stumbling into a green and pleasant land? Was that his eventual discovery of the Hollow Earth? When did all that "high strangeness" kick in?

Swartz: That "high strangeness" kicked in with his book "The Secret Lost Diaries of Admiral Byrd," which alleged that in 1947 he was conducting a flight over the northern polar areas. Actually, he was at the South Pole with Operation High Jump. There's this kind of curious discrepancy here.

Question: So he was at the North Pole in secret? The world didn't know he was there?

Swartz: Possibly. My speculation is that this alleged "secret diary" was actually released in a disinformation campaign to draw attention away from what was happening with Operation High Jump. Because whatever happened in Antarctica with Operation High Jump, it was decided that the information was important and had to be kept secret. Especially in the late 1950s and on into the 1960s, when a lot of information about Operation High Jump was starting to leak out a little bit, I think this book, "Secret Lost Diaries," had been written in an attempt to discredit the whole scenario.

We've seen that, again, with the UFO phenomenon, where the military, the government, intelligence officials – who knows? – have released information that is a little bit true and a lot false. The false part is so wild and crazy that it then tends to discredit everything. And that may be what is going on with this, that this whole story about Byrd flying over the North Pole and seeing areas of forest and prehistoric creatures and warm, almost tropical areas, having flown into the Hollow Earth – this may actually have been part of a campaign to discredit the stories that were starting to leak out concerning Operation High Jump. If you have these obviously wild stories of Byrd flying into the Hollow Earth and then juxtapose them with Operation High Jump, then people are going to disbelieve them both.

So if the stories come out that the Operation High Jump expedition found some kind of Nazi enclave in Antarctica and then had to come back to the U.S. extremely quickly, that's information that you don't want to leak out. So you go and combine that, then, with the Hollow Earth story where Byrd's plane was basically shanghaied by flying discs with swastikas on them, taken into the Hollow Earth and then given a meeting with the Hollow Earth people and being told basically the same kinds of stories that the UFO contactees were being told. That they were afraid of our atomic experiments and that if we persisted with them we were going to destroy ourselves. Then they possibly may have to come out from their secret cities underground and take over to stop us from doing that.

BYRD'S WARNING AND THE DAWN OF THE MODERN UFO ERA

I don't know. I really do think that the whole Hollow Earth part of this story is manufactured, that it did not happen like the popular stories have it. Instead it's being used to cover up whatever it was that happened to Byrd and his expedition Operation High Jump in Antarctica. Because when Byrd came back to the U.S., he was extremely concerned. He warned that the U.S. should adopt measures to protect us from the possibility of an invasion by hostile planes and missiles coming from the Polar Regions. He said he wasn't trying to scare us, but the cruel reality was that, in the case of a new war, the U.S. could be attacked by enemies flying over one or both poles. He gave a talk to Congress, and this was a secret talk. It was recorded that he gave this talk, but no transcripts have ever been released of just exactly what Byrd told the House and Senate during this official enquiry into what had happened in Antarctica. I don't think it's a coincidence as well that later that year, in July 1947, some kind of unusual aircraft crashed at Roswell.

A lot of present day writers will say that Byrd was afraid that Russia or China would send missiles or fly planes over the poles to attack the U.S. He didn't say that. He just warned against "enemies" attacking us FROM – he didn't say FLYING OVER – he said FROM the North or South Pole. Something happened that spooked him, but what that is, who knows? That's the whole conundrum about all of this. They weren't spooked like they'd been attacked and ships sank and planes crashed and personnel were killed. That didn't happen. But they were spooked enough that they left really early and then came back and warned the U.S. about some kind of invasion coming from the Polar Regions. And then, just a few months later, the whole modern UFO era started. And then you have the crash at Roswell of whatever that was. In the early days of the UFO mystery, especially with the crash at Roswell, the idea of this being extraterrestrial aircraft was not talked about. Instead there was the fear that these were Nazi aircraft or Nazi aircraft that had been found and were now being flown by the Soviet Union. It wasn't until later the whole extraterrestrial hypothesis started to come out.

So I think that a lot of these stories that deal with Byrd allegedly discovering an entranceway into the Hollow Earth are cover stories to deflect what was really going on. And I can only speculate about what was really going on, but I think it does have something to do with the Nazis and Nazi secret weapons. Whether or not they did discover a secret base in Antarctica, or maybe a small one – because I think the main operations were taking place out of South America. Especially in Argentina, where the Peron government was extremely friendly to the Nazis. A lot of Nazis escaped to Argentina at the end of the war, including lots of Nazi scientists who were in Argentina actually working to reestablish a Fourth Reich. We do know that they were trying to develop atomic weapons and they were also continuing their flying disc operations. It could very well be that the whole Antarctic thing was a misdirection.

One other thing that I should add to all this is that in 1968, even though there was an international provision not to conduct atomic tests in Antarctica, the U.S. exploded at least one and possibly several nuclear weapons in Antarctica in the areas where it had been alleged that these Nazi bases were located. And, again, that's one of these things where they weren't supposed to do that, the information was kind of occluded, but they did. It's rife for speculation. But why would the U.S. explode an atomic weapon in Antarctica when international treaties forbid it?

DID THE NAZIS STEAL TECHNOLOGY FROM NIKOLA TESLA?

Question: Recently you and publisher/author Tim Beckley produced a book "Nazi UFO Time Travelers." In this very intriguing title you bring up the idea that the Germans who came over under Operation Paperclip might have created a secret space program that might have been responsible for several UFO crashes – including the one outside of Roswell. How did you go about developing this theory and are some of the UFOs seen in our sky the results of Nazi handiwork?

Swartz: Operation Paperclip was the secret U.S. program in which more than 1,600 German scientists, engineers, and intelligent officers were recruited and brought to the United States for government employment from post-Nazi Germany. The primary purpose for Operation Paperclip was for the U.S. to gain a military and science advantage over the Soviet Union. Even though President Truman issued orders that no Germans who were Nazis during the war be allowed into, or to work for, the U.S., Operation Paperclip overruled that order and turned a blind eye to the fact that most who were brought to the U.S. had been (and probably still were) Nazis.

German scientists had made some amazing leaps in scientific knowledge during WWII, including the development of highly advanced aircraft and possibly even ships that could travel outside of Earth's atmosphere. The Nazis had a spy ring established on the East coast of the U.S. just before and during the war. One branch of this clandestine organization was dedicated to finding and stealing new and developing technology that could prove useful in their wartime effort. One notable prize that they were able to make off with was a sizable cache of notes and papers from Nikola Tesla. It appears that Germany was able to develop field propulsion technology from Tesla's early experiments and use this to develop a new form of aircraft that may have been responsible for some of the early UFO sightings around the world.

There were reports from Allied servicemen who were tasked with finding and identifying secret Nazi technology. Among this material that had been shipped back to the U.S. were strange disc-shaped aircraft that looked nothing like conventional planes or V-2 rockets. Apparently, some of the German scientists who had been brought to the U.S. had heard about these flying discs, but none had worked on their development. When UFOs began to be sighted starting in 1947, it was assumed that these were being flown by remnants of the Third Reich who had managed to escape to secret locations in Antarctica and South America. After these "UFOs" had been recovered by the U.S. military, there was a radical jump in scientific understanding on what we now call anti-gravity. Unfortunately, this scientific development has been kept secret from the civilian sector and more-than-likely has been used exclusively by the military.

After the crash at Roswell (and several other locations), the rumor began to circulate that UFOs were extraterrestrial spaceships. However, this may have been a disinformation campaign to hide the fact that UFOs were manmade, secret technology aircraft being operated by Germans who were attempting to establish the

Fourth Reich. Of course, Walter Bosley has done some excellent research on the idea that the development of secret, non-conventional aircraft can be traced as far back as the middle of the 19th century by a Bavarian group run almost like a secret society. This group may be one of two "breakaway civilizations" that have been operating on the fringes of our society for years.

GERMAN-SPEAKING ARYAN ALIENS

Question: Isn't it true that some of the early contactees claim the "space people" they met spoke with a German accent? Didn't the boot print of the man from Venus George Adamski claims to have met have the imprint of a swastika on the bottom of the sole? Were some of these contactees unknowingly having encounters with Nazi engineers?

Swartz: One of the curious things about the early contactees were their descriptions of the "Space Brothers," which almost invariably were tall, fair-skinned, blue-eyed and blond. This was the epitome of the Nazi belief of the perfect Aryan person. One of the first contactees, George Adamski, achieved national fame when he began to have visits from the Space Brothers who wanted him to be their spokesman. They told him they were from Venus and stressed the importance of stopping all nuclear testing and living in peace and harmony. Once, Adamski overheard the Space Brothers speaking to each other in fluent German. Being from Poland, he spoke some German, and easily recognized it as such. When he questioned the Brothers they answered that they spoke all the languages of Earth. Adamski and other contactees also said that alien writing they saw onboard the flying saucers looked remarkably like the old Nordic alphabet...including the swastika.

Then you had the Nebraskan Farm-Broker, Reinhold Schmidt, who on November 5, 1957, encountered a UFO that caused his car to break down out in the middle of nowhere. The landed UFO, which Schmidt described as looking like a "half-filled balloon," shot out a beam of light that struck him in the middle of his chest, causing instant paralysis. Schmidt was taken inside the craft where there were six occupants who spoke English with a German accent.

Schmidt would later write that when the occupants spoke among themselves they used High German, which he happened to understand. What is interesting is that Schmidt did not consider his experience as a contact with extraterrestrials; he thought that the ship was Russian, manned by a group of German scientists. After going to the authorities about his experience, a press release was issued stating that a "spaceship" had landed near Kearney, Nebraska. This surprised Schmidt since he had said nothing about seeing a spaceship. Afterwards, after being interviewed by two Air Force officers, Schmidt was taken in front of a mental competency board and committed to a psychiatric hospital. Apparently, the Air Force was not happy that Schmidt reported seeing Germans in a UFO and not spacemen from the planet Venus.

Question: How did the Nazis go about developing time travel, if they have it? I understand they had a team of female mediums who were channeling Aryan space beings as early as 1919.

Swartz: The idea that Germany may have achieved anti-gravity technology before and during WWII seems pretty amazing. But the idea that they may have also been able to take the first steps towards workable time travel is almost unbelievable. Before Hitler came to power, National Socialists had been developing projects meant to find the origins of the Aryans and the location of legendary Shamballa. They expected to obtain some secret knowledge to seize domination over the world. Secret expeditions were sent to Tibet and the Himalayas, and the number of such expeditions increased when the Nazis came to power in 1933.

The secret projects were especially active in the years 1935-1939, and probably continued even after the war campaign in Europe started. But all the documents pertaining to the projects were destroyed before Nazi Germany capitulated or possibly are still being kept hidden in undisclosed places.

FEMALE PSYCHICS CHANNELING FOR A NAZI FUTURE

It has been suggested that some Nazi expedition came across a wrecked UFO and contacted its crew somewhere along the line. Others speculate that contacts between Germans and extraterrestrials happened much earlier. In the early 1900s, "The All German Society for Metaphysics" (Alldeutsche Gesellschaft fr Metaphysik) were a group of woman spirit mediums who were involved in extraterrestrial telepathic contact. The society was later renamed the "Vril Society" or "Society of Vrilerinnen Women." The head of this group was Maria Orsitsch, who claimed that in 1917 she made contact with extraterrestrials from a distant solar system called Aldebaran.

Maria said that she received, via medium transmissions, technical data for the construction of a circular flight machine. In late November 1924, Maria Orsitsch visited Rudolf Hess in his apartment in Munich and revealed that they were already in the process of building a spacecraft based on this channeled information. Because of the sanctions placed on Germany after WWI, parts to build their spacecraft were slow to come in. This difficulty continued with the rise of Hitler and the Nazi Party, who placed a ban on secret societies in 1941.

In December 1943 Maria attended a secret meeting at the seaside resort of Kolberg. The main purpose of the meeting was to deal with the Aldebaran project. The Vril mediums had received precise information regarding the habitable planets around the Aldebaran sun and they were willing to plan a trip there. By 1944, high-ranking Nazi officials had been brought into the fold, and in January, there was a meeting between Hitler, Himmler, and Dr. W. Schumann (scientist and professor in the Technical University of Munich) where it was decided that a Vril 7

SECRET EXPLOITS OF ADMIRAL RICHARD E. BYRD

Jaeger spaceship would attempt a flight to Aldebaran.

The Vril 7 Jaeger spaceship was allegedly able to circumnavigate the speed of light by warping time-space. Essentially, it was a time machine. A test flight in late 1944 apparently almost ended in disaster as the ship returned damaged and "looking as if it had been flying for hundreds of years."

Not much is known after this point. Maria Orsitsch disappeared and there are only rumors about what happened to the Vril 7 Jaeger spaceship. The Nazi "Bell" may have been an independent development by the German military to weapon-ize time travel using the Vril Societies channeled information.

No one can say for sure if the Nazis actually had contacts with aliens or not. Defense technology and economy experts state that, at the end of the 1930s, Germany possessed just 57 submarines, and over the four years of WWII it built 1,163 modern, technologically-advanced submarines at its dockyards and even put them into operation. How was that possible when Germans were short of materials for waging war, and under the condition of terrible bombing by Allied forces? One may also wonder why Nazis did not create more perfect technologies with the assistance of extraterrestrial intellect. In fact, the Germans used only technologies that required a short production period.

Nazis created the first jet-propelled aircraft that could make up to 1,000 km/h and was superior to any airplane known in the anti-Hitler coalition. It is a mystery how Germans managed to produce 2,000 new fighting machines over the few months of 1945.

As for manmade flying saucers, the U.S. war archives and the British Air Force archives contain a great number of reports from military pilots who said they came across strange flying apparatuses resembling British military helmets when flying over Germany. American Kenneth Arnold, who is known as the UFO "discoverer," was not the first contemporary who witnessed flying saucers in the sky. British and American pilots witnessed the phenomenon during WWII. Firing at such objects did not damage them at all!

On October 14, 1943, British Air Force Major R. Holmes reported that he witnessed several "big bright discs" during bombardment of Schweinfurt. And the objects did not respond to firing. Pilots of U.S. Air Force interceptors who flew over the German territory in the winter of 1945 also witnessed UFOs. These days, some authors insist that the above episodes prove that the Third Reich had secret weapons at its disposal. They also refer to German designers Schriever, Habermol, Miethe and Belluzzo, who were said to be working on flying discs since 1941. But reputable aviation experts denied this version. They said that even modern technologies did not allow production of aircraft as invulnerable and speedy as those objects. Indeed, the experts were absolutely right, but they did not consider the fact that Germans could have created the apparatuses after a contact with aliens.

SECRET EXPLOITS OF ADMIRAL RICHARD E. BYRD

WAS A NAZI THE WORLD'S FIRST ASTRONAUT?

Raul Streicher, 85, from Germany made a sensational statement in Der Spiegel in 2000. The old man insisted that it was he who was in fact the number one spaceman, not Soviet Yuri Gagarin! He added that he had been first in orbit in 1945. That sounded like an absolute fable, and Der Spiegel launched a special investigation of the case and studied classified archives of the Third Reich. The investigation proved that the old man was not lying.

Before WWII, Germany set up a network of secret research institutes to develop and improve arms and methods of impact on humans. In 1938, a specialized rocket engineering research institute was founded near Wewelsburgh where the SS headquarters were located. Reich's Marshal Gering was the curator of the institute that designed the panzerfaust, the Panzerknakke pocket grenade cup discharge and various war missiles, including the Fau-3 missile complex. Nazis pinned great hopes in the latter, as the A9/A10 cruise missile that was part of the complex could be used either as intercontinental (Hitler planned to destroy New York in the summer of 1945) or as a space rocket.

Test launching of the missile took place in 1943, but the invention turned out to be technically imperfect and sixteen out of the eighteen launched missiles exploded at take-off or in the air. Next year, the research institute produced about 40 improved missiles. At the same time, the Fuehrer ordered the recruitment of military astronauts among German aces. A new squadron consisting of from 100 to 500 pilots was formed in March 1944. Raul Streicher was also among them.

After several successful tests of the rockets in 1944, the final selection of astronauts was made. Hitler chose two candidates by referring to their personal horoscopes, as he was fond of astrology. Those were Martin von Dulen and Raul Streicher, and the Fuehrer obviously sympathized with the latter. A rocket with von Dulen onboard was first launched on February 18, 1945. The rocket exploded about three minutes after takeoff. In six days another rocket with Raul Streicher onboard was successfully launched, orbited the Earth and landed on water in Japan. So, Streicher says that his flight on February 24, 1945, was the beginning of space exploration by humans.

When the Nazis realized that their war campaign was lost they decided to blow up a small cosmo-drome near Wewelsburg and planned to shelter the results of their investigations and some of the scientists with the secret research institute in a castle in the Carpathian Mountains. The leader of the research institute was the owner of the castle and he hoped to continue researches there after the end of the war and some day gain revenge. But the sweeping advance of the Allied forces frustrated the plans. American forces seized the head of the research institute, and Soviet troops got some of the rockets designed by the institute. Later they were used in development of the Soviet space program.

SECRET EXPLOITS OF ADMIRAL RICHARD E. BYRD

There was an order to liquidate Streicher as he knew too much. The astronaut was in hiding in Eastern Europe for some time and then after several years settled in GDR. After Yuri Gagarin's first flight into space in 1961, Streicher announced that it was he and not the Soviet astronaut who must be considered the pioneer of space. However, the man failed to provide any evidence to prove that he was telling the truth.

Question: Did the Nazis ever get to the moon?

Swartz: After World War II, rumors circulated that German astronauts had traveled to the moon and established a top-secret facility there. There were several different aeronautical programs going on in Germany during WWII that involved disc-shaped craft. One was the Vril project I mentioned earlier that used a unique propulsion system to warp time and space. The other German projects researched conventional jet/rocket propulsion and field propulsion.

Question: I know Tim Beckley has posted his thought that some of the early UFO groups may have been trying to cover up a Nazi/UFO connection by pushing the theory that the flying saucers, if they existed, were from far off worlds. Do you think Major Keyhoe and the NICAP staff knew what was really going on and tried to divert attention from a more earthbound theory?

Swartz: I don't know. I think that the disinformation campaign about UFOs has been so successful over the years that we may never know the truth. There did seem to be an effort almost from the beginning to lead investigators away from any other possibility other than UFOs are extraterrestrial. That, or they are hoaxes and misidentifications of known objects. Any other explanation, like the idea that they are human-constructed, top secret aircraft/spacecraft, was always quickly discounted. This despite the fact that Army Air Force and Navy officers worried early on that UFOs were some sort of high technology of the Nazis or from the Soviet Union using captured Nazi equipment.

Question: After all is said and done, is the Earth hollow in your opinion? Ringed by a vast system of tunnels and chambers?

Swartz: I wish I could give a definitive answer to that question. I don't think the Earth is completely hollow, like it was imagined by Edgar Rice Burroughs in his Pellucidar series of books where the Earth is a hollow shell with the inner world as the internal surface of that shell. However, I have never been there, so I can't say for sure. I do believe that there are vast series of tunnels and large chambers throughout the planet, and that many seem to be thousands, if not millions, of years old. There have been hundreds of people throughout history that have visited these amazing structures and have made it back to tell about them. So I am inclined to believe that this is a fact.

* * * *

07

GOING DEEP UNDERGROUND TO EXPOSE
THE SECRET SPACE PROGRAM
By Timothy Green Beckley

Are some of the most fantastic unidentified objects that traverse through our atmosphere – going about their business mostly undetected – manufactured right here on earth?

Are these advanced "air ships" being constructed under our very noses, as part of some super-secret space program that the public has not been made aware of?

And if so, who is behind this unknown space program which has seemingly developed a craft – or several types of vehicles – that operate utilizing a highly advanced propulsion system that is obviously light years ahead of NASA's quite primitive efforts to take us to the moon and beyond?

Has some secret society or cabal, operating literally underground, back engineered a crashed UFO, perhaps in Germany sometime in the mid-1930s as reported? Or is this technology something that has been utilized for eons by a race of beings who go undetected living inside our planet?

Who indeed has developed a space program that produces craft that are so advanced in design and flight ability that they are capable of hovering silently over our communities, darting about utilizing all sorts of aerodynamically "impossible" maneuvers – as if they were special effects in a Star Wars movie? And then kicking into "warp speed" to cruise across space and time?

Furthermore, if such a highly advanced propulsion system has been developed why, is it being kept secret and hidden from the public? Is our right to take our legitimate place in some perceived "galactic federation" being hampered by an unknown group – originating underground or at the Poles? They are seemingly more concerned with their own financial gain, possible global conquest or keeping a strangle hold they have maintained for eons, enabling to keep us as human slaves and guinea pigs for sadistic purpose as represented in the doctrine of the Shaver Mystery.

No one can deny that Dr Michael E. Salla is a polarizing figure in what has become known as the Exopolitical movement. There are those who praise him as a communicator on behalf of extraordinarily unconventional interplanetary affairs that include relations with technologically advanced ETs, as well as an avatar of universal wisdom whose only goal is to disseminate what he sees as the truth about UFOs and the secret space program. Likewise, there are those that say he is anything from a "UFO gadfly" to one of the most gifted disinformation artists to go before the public. He truly has made a name for himself in a provocative field and people either approve of his conceptualization of cosmic matters – which are often of a highly doctrinal nature – or speculate that his approach to the universe at large is so farfetched that it is out of step with reality and brings ridicule to an emerging field that could potentially be important to each and every one of us soon enough.

The jury is out and you must be the ultimate judge, just as you are to be on the bulk of material revealed by numerous sources throughout this book.

Regardless of your reasoning on this issue, there is no doubt but that Dr. Salla is a charming, well-spoken individual who has kept audiences spellbound on programs like "Coast to Coast AM" and at pointedly liberal minded New Age and Metaphysical conferences that embrace the reality of time travel, alien bases on the moon, and even Nazi flying saucers.

But please allow Dr. Salla to describe himself, as displayed on his Exopolitics.org web site:

"Dr. Michael E. Salla is a pioneer in the development of 'Exopolitics,' the political study of the key actors, institutions and processes associated with extraterrestrial life. His interest in Exopolitics evolved out of his investigation of the sources of international conflict and its relationship to an extraterrestrial presence that is not acknowledged to the general public, elected officials or even senior military officials.

"Dr. Salla's groundbreaking 'Implications of the Extraterrestrial Presence' (2004) was the first published book on Exopolitics and explained the political implications of extraterrestrial life. In 'Exposing U.S. Government Policies on Extraterrestrial Life' (2009) he revealed how the world's most powerful nation secretly manages information concerning extraterrestrial life and technology. In 'Galactic Diplomacy: Getting to Yes with ET' (2013) he shows how humanity can negotiate with extraterrestrial civilizations in a way that protects our vital interests. He documents the tragic efforts by President Kennedy to share information more widely in 'ssination/dp/0982290268" Kennedy's Last Stand: Eisenhower, UFOs, MJ-12 & JFK's Assassination' and 'The Truth About UFOs and Extraterrestrial Visitation.' Finally, in his most recent book, 'Insiders Reveal Secret Space Programs And Extraterrestrial Alliances,' (2015), he analyzes whistle blower testimonies revealing the extent of classified space programs and extraterrestrial diplomacy."

And while he has many devoted fans and followers who praise him for what they say is his discriminating effort to reveal the truth about UFOs and the secret space program , there are likewise those that say he is anything from a "disclosure windbag" to one of the most gifted disinformation operatives to make a name for himself in the Exopolitical arena.

One would assume with Dr. Salla's "dicey resume" that he would be prone to be rather conservative in his approach to matters of Exopolitics. However, as a review of his archived papers indicates, this is far from the truth. Salla even seems to give kudos to the theory that at least some UFOs might "pop up" from some subterranean domain.

"A third constituency appears to be races of beings that inhabit Earth's subterranean realms. These subterranean races, or 'intra-terrestrials,' have been described as being both human descendants of ancient kingdoms such as Lemuria, and a non-human race that has reptilian characteristics. Evidence from a wide range of sources, including government whistle blowers, contactees and remote viewers, gives credence to the existence of such subterranean races that have technologies far more advanced than surface humanity. According to Brad Steiger, for example, 'these ancient human civilizations went underground many millennia ago.'"

THE NAZI AGENDA

Not one to hold anything back, Dr. Salla issued a position paper titled: "Foundations for Globally Managing Extraterrestrial Affairs – The Legacy of the Nazi Germany-Extraterrestrial Connection." While space does not permit us to reproduce the entire abstract, we do want to air at least an abridgment of his statement, thus the edited version of his copyright work which can be read in full off his website. . .

Introduction

"There is compelling evidence that in the early 1930's, the technology and presence of one or more extraterrestrial (ET) races became known to the leaders of Nazi Germany who embarked on an ambitious effort to communicate with these races for the purpose of acquiring their advanced technology. Using communication techniques that would be widely dismissed today as 'psychic channeling', there is evidence that the Nazi sponsorship of occult societies, that specialized in this form of communication with these ET races, was successful in gaining information that produced rapid technological breakthroughs that eventually came to the attention of the intelligence services of Britain, France, USSR and the USA. While predictably dismissive of such esoteric practices by the Nazi regime, each of the intelligence services of these major states initiated efforts to attain whatever intelligence information they could gain on the purported Nazi communication methods with an ET race(s) while monitoring the 'ET inspired' technology being developed by Nazi Germany.

"At a time of growing international tension, where another major European war (World War 2) loomed on the horizon, major global powers would have been concerned about the ramifications of Nazi Germany seeking to acquire advanced technology through esoteric forms of communication with ET races. While sightings of ET/UFO craft were relatively rare in the 1930's, historically there had been sufficient sightings to raise the possibility of an ET presence on the planet for political leaders. Not only was Nazi Germany actively developing technology that was inspired through such communication, but it had also learned of remote locations around the planet where it could retrieve ET artifacts. The Nazis sponsored numerous expeditions to remote locations the results of which were largely unknown to Western intelligence services.There is also evidence that Nazi Germany was able to eventually retrieve an operational 'ET craft', which suggested the Nazis were being assisted by one or more ET races.

* * * * *

NAZI GERMANY'S PREWAR PROGRAMS TO DEVELOP
ET-INSPIRED TECHNOLOGY

"Adolph Hitler's fascination with Occult Sciences, Esoteric philosophies and exotic technologies led him to exploiting whatever avenues he had in gaining access to and developing weapons technologies that would allow Nazi Germany to gain its rightful place, in Hitler's view, as a leading global power. As a student of occult sciences, Hitler was well aware of the possibility of communicating with extraterrestrial races through methods such as 'psychic channeling' whereby an individual could establish communication with non-physical and/or distant life forms and transmit information. Such communication was well known among the Occult societies scattered throughout Northern Europe who studied the work of mystics such as Helena Blavatsky. She who wrote extensively of her esoteric communications with other 'life forms' and how to develop these communication abilities.

"While such a phenomenon in the contemporary era struggles to be taken seriously by the general public, there is compelling evidence that not only did Hitler take it seriously, but devoted considerable resources of the Nazi state into converting information gained from such efforts into technology development and weapons production. Much of the information gained in such 'psychic communications' led to Nazi expeditions in the period before the Second World War to remote locations such as Tibet, Antarctica, South America, Iraq and elsewhere in search of buried ET artifacts from earlier civilizations.

"One of the principal Nazi occult societies that were supported by Hitler was the Vril Society that "was allegedly 'channeling' messages from an alien civilization in the Aldebaran solar system and planned to develop a craft that could make physical contact with the civilization there." Another significant Occult Group was the Thule Society that was similarly claiming to be in communication with an advanced race; rather than an off-world ET race However, this was an advanced human race with Nordic features from an ancient Earth civilization that inhabited subterranean territories. These territories were accessible from the Polar Regions and other secluded areas around the planet.

"The seriousness and support given by Hitler to such communications is evidenced by the material support given to these Occult societies in terms of scientific resources for developing their 'ET inspired' technologies. By 1934, for example, "the Vril Society had apparently developed its first UFO shaped aircraft, known as the Vril 1, which was propelled by an anti-gravity effect. While there was predictable skepticism by more traditional branches of the German military of the viability of such 'channeled' information, the Nazi SS were at the forefront of efforts to develop this technology. Later in the Second World War, the Nazi SS would take over complete control of Hitler's 'scientific-military-occult complex' ensuring the highest level of secrecy in developing and operationalising ET inspired technology."

THE NAZI RETREAT TO ANTARCTICA,
'OPERATION HIGH JUMP' AND ET ASSISTANCE

"The 'official' defeat of Nazi Germany and Imperial Japan in 1945 was in fact a 'tactical victory' that masked a major strategic defeat for the 'victorious Allies' that was kept from the general public. A significant proportion of Nazi Germany's political elite, their most advanced ET technology and fully operational 'saucer ships' had escaped from Allied occupation forces. What remained was Nazi Germany's advanced weapons programs which were disturbing enough in terms of the overall technological advances achieved by the Nazis in many fields of arms production. The fact that the Nazis had removed their most advanced secrets, technology and personnel during the run up to the final defeat of Germany, would have been a huge shock to Allied leaders once it became clear what had occurred. Rather than the final months of the Second World War being a last desperate gamble by a megalomaniac Nazi leadership that could not accept inevitable defeat, it was in fact a holding action for a methodically well planned extraction of the Nazi's most valuable resources and personnel to well-prepared remote locations in the Antarctic and South America. This allowed the Nazis to continue their unique social system, and plan to eventually play an important, if not dominant, role in global affairs."

For purposes of continuity we have removed the prevailing footnotes and request that those who hold an advanced interest in Exopolitcs and the possible Nazi – ET connection go directly to Salla's site for a more thorough discussion of the issue.

SUGGESTED READING – BOOKS BY DR. SALLA

GALACTIC DIPLOMACY: GETTING TO YES WITH ET

INSIDERS REVEAL SECRET SPACE PROGRAMS AND EXTRATERRESTRIAL ALLIANCES

KENNEDY'S LAST STAND: EISENHOWER, UFOS, MJ-12 AND JFK'S ASSASSI-NATION

Dr. Michael Salla

08

A BRITISH EARL, THE HOLLOW EARTH
AND THE LOST UNDERGROUND TUNNEL SYSTEM OF ATLANTIS
By Timothy Green Beckley

I guess I've always made friends fairly easy.

Not that I am an overly outward-going kind of guy. When you first meet me I can be kind of shy, but I do open up after a while and I guess I let my true feelings show. And I do have a goddamn sense of humor, sometimes in a sick sort of way (afterhours I play the character Mr. Creepo in a series of positively B-grade horror movies such as "Blood Sucking Vampire Freaks").

When I was still a kid living with my parents in New Jersey I started a mimeographed UFO newsletter which was called "The Interplanetary News Service Report." The name is sort of self-explanatory – in those days, if you believed in UFOs, you more or less accepted the fact that they had to come from somewhere

Lord Brinsley Le Poer Trench, Eight Earl of Clancarty

in outer space. It was like the live version of "The Day The Earth Stood Still," if you thought all aliens benign, or "Invasion of the Body Snatchers" if you grappled with the concept these "monsters" were here to invade our Godforsaken world. Most of us hadn't thought of Nazi-developed discs or giants from the Hollow Earth, and those who knew about the supposed subterranean exploits of that mad writer, Richard Shaver, thought he had gone totally bonkers with his talk of the sinister "dero," who he said inhabited the caverns below our feet.

As "The Interplanetary News Service Report" gained respectability, we

Brinsley Le Poer Trench in Japan

began branching out from just an American-based publication to one with a worldwide circulation, exchanging information and communications with over one hundred groups and their appointed representatives in Europe, Asia and South America. One gentlemen eager to correspond and exchange reports of UFOs with my group was a member of Britain's House of Lords: Brinsley Le Poer Trench, who had been winning international recognition in the field of UFOlogy for a number of years. From 1956 to 1959, Trench edited the very prestigious "Flying Saucer Review" and founded the International Unidentified Object Observer Corps. In 1967, he organized Contact International and served as its first president. He also served as vice-president of the British UFO Research Association (BUFORA).

In 1975 he succeeded to the earldom on the death of his half-brother, giving him a seat in the British Parliament as the 8th Earl of Clancarty. He used his new position to found a UFO study group at the House of Lords, introducing "Flying Saucer Review" to its library and pushing for the declassification of UFO data several decades before the term "Disclosure" with a big "D" became a common term for the release of all documents on the subject proving that UFOs were real and extraterrestrial in origin. After taking up his official position, the Earl organized a celebrated debate in the House of Lords which elicited many speeches on the question of UFO reality, both pro and con. He even began to invite researchers from other countries to appear before the group to discuss the matter and broaden the scope of the organization, which they hoped would get Her Majesty's government to come clean about what it knew on this fascinating and perplexing subject of flying saucers (still known to some under this moniker instead of the more recent term, UFO).

For many years I had a long-distance friendship with Brinsley, now the 8th Earl of Clancarty, until eventually he requested my presence in London to air my personal position on UFOs for the members of what certainly had to be considered one of the most prestigious groups in the world, with its "by special invitation only" membership roll.

GETTING UP CLOSE AND PERSONAL WITH THE EARL

Long before Brinsley invited me to London to speak before the House Of Lords UFO group, I had been in regular correspondence with the hardworking Briton. Just like I had done, he'd developed a worldwide chain of correspondence in an era long before it was possible to email someone and have them receive your message in mere seconds. It sometimes took weeks to receive a handwritten letter that was actually penned on a very lightweight blue paper and folded over into a self-mailer and then sent across the pond to an American correspondent like myself, who anxiously awaited the arrival of the latest saucer intelligence from the land of Her Majesty.

From what he had written me and from mutual friends on both sides of the Atlantic, I fully realized that Brinsley was known for making some fairly bombastic statements which made him somewhat of an "outcast" to those that represented the "nuts-and-bolts" wing of UFOlogy, with their prevailing belief that all unidentified flying objects had to be from outer space and represented an advanced technology. They stubbornly contended that there was nothing paranormal about their behavior, that they were just one step ahead of us in the scientific department.

The unflappable Earl was by no means tied down to such a simplistic approach to our flying friends. He certainly was not trapped in the "here and now," claiming to having traced his family tree back thousands of years to the time when aliens first landed on Earth. He told me that during WW II he had read of several incidents in which our fastest military aircraft were followed by what became known as "the foo fighters," craft which could not be attributed to either the Allied or Axis forces and for which there was no rational explanation. Upon discussing the topic with others in the early 1950s, it was thought that there was a need for a

SECRET EXPLOITS OF ADMIRAL RICHARD E. BYRD

good UFO publication, and thus the prestigious "Flying Saucer Review" was created and distributed to those with a thirst for knowledge on a cosmic level.

Quite a few years ahead of Erich Von Daniken in his belief in ancient astronauts, Brinsley was able to give up his regular job selling ad space for a magazine on gardening when his first book, "The Sky People," (now available in an updated edition as "Legacy Of The Sky People") started to sell at a more-than-modest level. Around this time, Trench joined forces with a Japanese UFO contactee group that published an English language magazine called "Brothers."

The newly-merged group was initially known as the International Sky Scouts. Brinsley also traveled to Japan, where he spoke before several gatherings mainly attended by members of the "Japanese UFO youth movement." Eventually, the group had to change its name after being drawn into a lawsuit by the real Boy Scouts, who saw Brinsley's use of the organization's name as an infringement on their organization's trademark.

As a "compromise," the name was changed to Contact International, which continues to issue "Awareness," a quarterly journal which Brinsley started decades back. And while Brinsley had started out as a literal believer in the ETH , short for the "extraterrestrial hypothesis," he told me out in the foyer when we met at the House of Lords, where I was to deliver my talk, that he had changed his opinion and now believed that UFOs were part of an underground civilization which had established a tunnel system from one end of the Earth to another, thus enabling them to move around unimpeded.

In short, Brinsley thought this Inner Earth society was well ahead of ours in many respects and had learned to live in peace since its original downfall during the time of Atlantis when it had first gone underground. He also saw its technology as being hundreds of years more advanced, leaning on various forms of fossil-free fuel to sail their ships about upon emerging from their secretive quarters located miles underground.

No doubt the Earl was scoffed at behind his back as this was certainly a radical theory even for the most dedicated UFOlogist, who thought themselves open-minded, but spent most of their time wearing blinders which prevented them

SECRET EXPLOITS OF ADMIRAL RICHARD E. BYRD

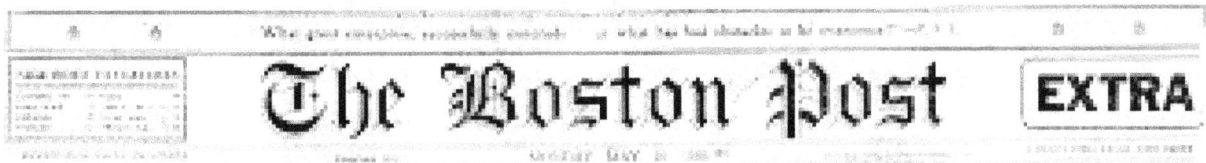

The Boston Post EXTRA

BYRD FLIES TO POLE AND RETURNS SAFELY

Marvelous Feat by U. S. Navy Flier—Makes 1200-Mile Trip From Spitsbergen to North Pole and Return in 15 1-2 Hours—Chief Petty Officer Bennett of Navy With Him as Mechanic—Average Speed Just 80 Miles an Hour

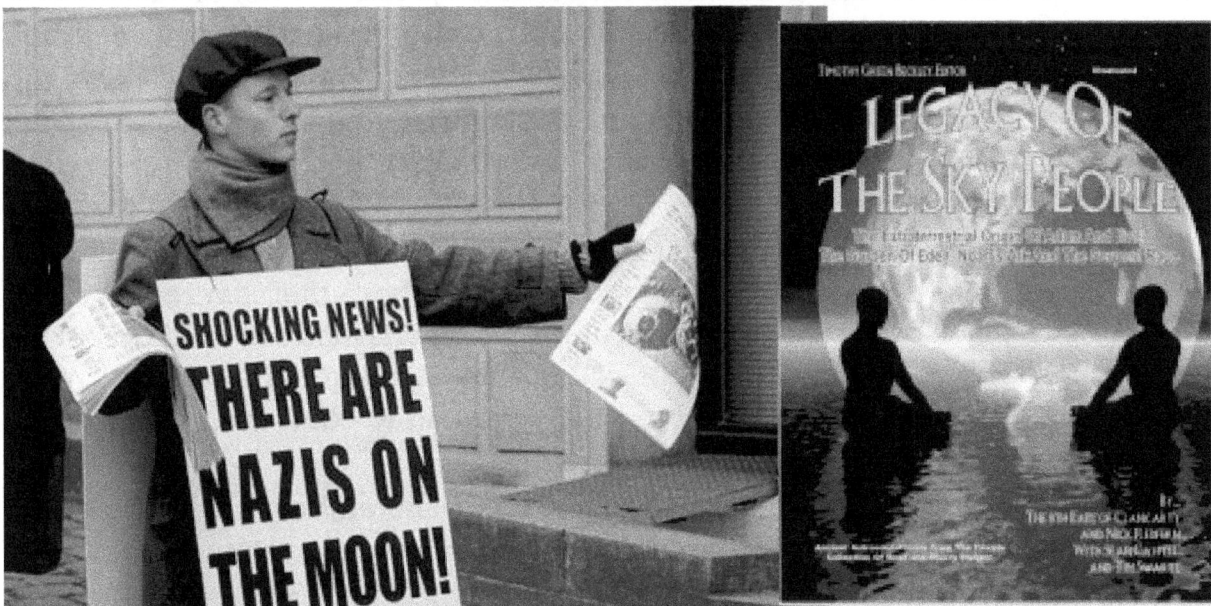

SHOCKING NEWS! THERE ARE NAZIS ON THE MOON! ...ABOUT IT!

Truth Today

CONTACT INTERNATIONAL UFO RESEARCH

AWARENESS

JULY 2015 VOLUME 34 No 3
+ Pluto - The Final Frontier
+ Rendlesham - New Facts

LEGACY OF THE SKY PEOPLE

Photo # NH 101037 Loening OL-2 amphibian on flight during Cuban survey duty, circa 1926

Byrd's Loening NA-4 Amphibian

from taking in newly emerging independent theories. Put simply – they were not about to rock the boat and go against what they saw as the scientific grain, not that science considered them as peers anyway. It was still all   hocus pocus to those bearing academic degrees from "accredited" universities and "houses of recognizable letters."

THE ATLANTIS TUNNEL SYSTEM EXPLORED

Being the authorized publisher of Trench's "Finding Lost Atlantis Inside The Hollow Earth" – essentially an updated version of the original British paperback released as "Secret Of The Ages" – we thought it relevant that we present a few of Brinsley's "unconventional" ideas about the great unsolved mysteries surrounding the possibility of an Inner Earth, lost worlds and the holes at the poles, complete with a central sun in the middle of the Earth.

Trench said that they – the Atlanteans – while still living on the surface of the planet – had built awe-inspiring megalithic buildings like the city of Tiahuanaco, which was constructed in an unusual manner in order to make it earthquake proof.

"The world," noted Brinsley, "in those far-off days was physically very unstable. For this reason, too, the Atlanteans built fantastic tunnel systems in which refuge could be taken, if necessary, from both the onslaughts of nature and attacks from outer space."

Erich von Daniken claimed that he knew about such a tunnel system underneath Ecuador and Peru which led into a huge hall where there were stone and metal objects, including statues of many kinds of animals made of solid gold. Furthermore, there was a metal library consisting of metal plaques (leaves) with writing on them in an unknown language, which are said to contain a history of humanity and details about a vanished civilization.

There is some disagreement as to how von Daniken became aware of this information and if he visited the tunnel and saw the tunnel system and gold for himself.

Part of the puzzle may be clarified later in 2017 with the release of a documentary film produced by Debora Goldstern, who has authored a 400-page book in Spanish on the secrets of the caverns of Ecuador and the possible existence of their supposed fabulous golden contents.

"Sources contend that the builders of the tunnels used a combination of thermal drills and electron ray guns."

A farfetched idea? Except for the fact that for the last several decades the U.S. military has used high-tech boring machines to dig tunnels deep beneath the Earth, turning some of these tunnels into research facilities. The one we hear about the most has its entrance located high in the foothills outside the town of Dulce, New Mexico. UFO sightings, the appearance of black – unmarked – helicopters and cattle mutilations have previously been connected to this rumored facility.

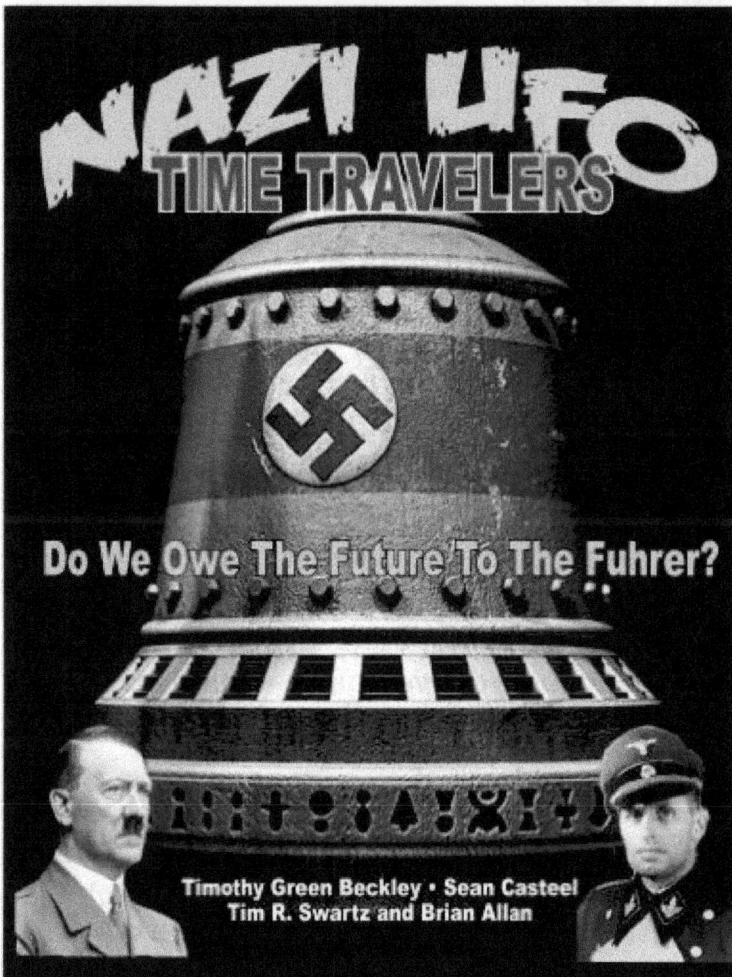

Advanced anti-gravity flying disks and "Die Glock" time travel device. Just a few of the marvelous machines claimed to have been built by the Germans during and after World War Two.

SECRET EXPLOITS OF ADMIRAL RICHARD E. BYRD

Amongst Brinsley's most credited and seemingly knowledgeable sources is Italy's Peter Kokosimo, the pseudonym of Pier Domenico Colosimo. He was born in Modena, and lived in ia.org/wiki/Bolzano"Bolzano, Turin and Milan. In 1969 he won the Premio Bancarella, one of Italy's most prestigious literary prizes, for *Non è terrestre* ("Not of this World"). His books have been translated in 60 countries, including Russia, Japan and China. Kolosimo also founded and coordinated the Italian Association for Prehistoric Studies.

Kolosimo pointed out that a mysterious series of tunnel systems is to be found all over the world. Apart from South America, he listed California, Virginia, Hawaii, Oceania and Asia. In Europe there are tunnels in Sweden and Czechoslovakia; and, in the Mediterranean area, in the Balearics and Malta. He added: "A huge tunnel, some thirty miles of which have been explored, runs between Spain and Morocco, and many believe that this is how the 'Barbary Apes,' which are otherwise unknown in Europe, reached Gibraltar."

Indeed, Kolosimo wrote: "It has even been suggested that these Cyclopean galleries form a network connecting the most distant parts of our planet." Peter said he was curious to know who had constructed the tunnels that lead out under the sea on Easter Island, and for what purpose.

Another source, the British archaeologist Harold T. Wilkins, has more to tell us about the ancient tunnel systems:

Among the Mongolian tribes of Inner Mongolia, even today, there are traditions about tunnels and subterranean worlds which sound as fantastic as anything in modern novels. One legend – if it be that! – says that the tunnels lead to a subterranean world of antediluvian descent somewhere in a recess of Afghanistan or in the region of the Hindu Kush . . .

It is even given a name – Agharti (most commonly spelled Agharta). The legend adds that a labyrinth of tunnels and underground passages is extended in a series of links connecting Agharti with all other such subterranean worlds! The subterranean world, it is said, is lit by a strange green luminescence which favors the growth of crops and is conducive to length of days and health.

This last account is, comments Trench, of special interest, as Peter Kolosirno refers to this green fluorescence in another part of the world. He writes about a strange "bottomless well" in Azerbaijan in the Soviet Union. Apparently, a bluish light comes from its wall and odd noises are heard. Eventually, after investigating and exploring, scientists found a whole system of tunnels connecting with other ones in Georgia and all over the Caucasus.

After describing these tunnels, which are regular in form, and, he stated, almost identical with similar ones in Central America, Kolosimo went on to tell us that they are part of a huge system connecting with Iran and, moreover, with the tunnels of China, Tibet and Mongolia.

SECRET EXPLOITS OF ADMIRAL RICHARD E. BYRD

Now, referring back to Harold T. Wilkins' account of a subterranean world called Agharti, which was said to be lit by a strange green luminescence, Kolosimo has this to say:

The Tibetans believe that the tunnels are citadels, the last of which will afford refuge to the survivors of an immense cataclysm. This unknown people is said to make use of an underground source of energy which replaces that of the sun, causing plants to breed and prolonging human life. It is supposed to give out a green fluorescence, and it is curious that we also meet with this idea in American legend.

Apparently, the Atlanteans built tunnel systems all over the world for several purposes. First, to protect themselves from the very common onslaughts of nature in the form of seismic activity and floods, and, secondly, as a protection if attacked from outer space. The degree of advanced technology to match the tunnel boring feats of this ancient civilization, Brinsley indicates, would be almost impossible when even using modern day scientific methods.

A SUBSTANTIAL CASE FOR THE EARTH BEING HOLLOW

When push comes to shove, Brinsley's "Hail Mary" seems to be his contention that the world IS positively hollow. That there are openings around the globe. And that people much like us are going about their business way down below where curious eyes cannot pry.

His way of thinking is that the UFO occupants are deliberately attempting to put us off the track regarding their point of origin.

"Over the last few years, many UFO researchers, including myself, had come around to the view that most of the UFO activity emanated from an invisible area interpenetrating our planet, rather than from the old widely accepted extraterrestrial point of origin. This viewpoint came about to some extent through the ability of both the UFOs and the UFOnauts to materialize and dematerialize, and perform many other feats, pointing to the probability that they emerged into our plane of existence from another order of matter. That is, from an invisible realm."

In addition to the possibility that UFO entities manipulate a good deal of psychic phenomena to get themselves here, Brinsley says that, "Many UFOlogists consider that the 'aliens' pretend to come from Mars, Venus, Jupiter and all stopover points out in space, so as to confuse us and not disclose their real place of residence. It is just possible that they materialize and dematerialize, teleport people and bring out poltergeist activity for the same reason. In short, to confuse us still further and put into our minds the idea of an invisible realm as their habitat. Simply put, perhaps we are being deliberately put off the track.

"The answer," the late member of the House of Lords concludes, "may lie literally beneath our feet! If a race of people are living in the interior of the Earth, then they would have been resident there for at least 12,000 years."

SECRET EXPLOITS OF ADMIRAL RICHARD E. BYRD

While hardly an original concept these days, when one considers the variety of material now available on the Hollow Earth hypothesis. But this was an earlier time, when Brinsley had just begun to contemplate the idea that there is a secret space program operated by a hidden race of beings that are trying to keep themselves invisible. Trench reported on these important "facts" he wanted everyone to consider:

(1) Throughout history, numerous polar explorers found that when they got to the farthest northern regions of the polar area, the weather got warmer. What is the alternative answer to stating that this was caused by warm air blowing up through the polar entrance?

(2) Polar explorers in the far north have come across a warm sea. Why should this be?

(3) Abundant game and animal life have been discovered in these farthest north regions. Nansen was puzzled by the fox-trails. Warm-blooded animals in that area were beyond his comprehension. The only answer seems to be that they came out of the interior of the Earth.

(4) Now here is probably one of the most important questions of all. Why did Nansen find that in the farthest north area, the north-south horizon became foreshortened while the east-west one remained constant? Surely, this meant that he had gone over the lip of the "hole" and was beginning to descend very gradually into the interior.

(5) If you were traveling down into the interior of the Earth, instead of proceeding horizontally on the Earth's surface, the compass needle must point up towards the North Magnetic Pole, rather than north, as it did while travelling on the surface. This is what happened in the case of Nansen. Surely, another indication that he went a little way down into the interior.

(6) Why is there so much dust in the Arctic? It has been known to float around in great clouds and fall on ships. Nansen complained bitterly about this dust. It causes the snow on which it falls to turn black. This dust has been analyzed and found to be composed of carbon and iron; it is supposed to come out of some volcano. There are no volcanoes in the Arctic, so the only place the dust could conceivably come from is a volcano inside the Earth, blown up through the entrance.

Obviously, only man will decide the outcome of the debate as to the earth being hollow or not. Academia is not likely to say they have been wrong all this time in their physical configuration of our world. They might as well just go back and accept the concept of a Flat Earth while they are at it!

But certainly the 8th Earl of Clancarty, our old friend Brinsley Le Poer Trench, might have opened a few nimble minds and shown us all that sometimes our thinking can be more primitive than those starry-eyed people who once inhabited the

SECRET EXPLOITS OF ADMIRAL RICHARD E. BYRD

surface but may now live far below and way underground.

SUGGESTED READING, BOOKS BY BRINSLEY LE POER TRENCH

FINDING LOST ATLANTIS INSIDE THE HOLLOW EARTH

LEGACY OF THE SKY PEOPLE: THE EXTRATERRESTRIAL ORIGIN OF ADAM AND EVE; THE GARDEN OF EDEN; NOAH'S ARK AND THE SERPENT RACE

Peter and Caterina Kolosimo at their home in Torino, Italy

Hanebau Two and Hanebau One anti-gravity disks.

Various models of
Vril flying saucers

Vril Nazi UFOs

09

UNDERGROUND CITIES OF THE INNER EARTH
Dr. R. W. Bernard, B.A., M.A., Ph.D.

We have indicated previously that the subterranean cities of Agharta were constructed by Atlanteans as refugees from the radioactive fallout produced by the nuclear war they fought, and also referred to Huguenin's theory that flying saucers were Atlantean aircraft which were brought to the Subterranean World prior to the occurrence of the catastrophe that sank Atlantis. The abandonment of their former home on top of the four-sided sacred mountain in the center of Atlantis (Mount Olympus or Meru, later memorialized by the four-sided, truncated pyramids of Egypt and Mexico) and their skyward journey over the Rainbow Bridge of the Aurora Borealis, through the polar opening, to the new home in Valhalla, the golden palaces of the city of Shamballah, capital of Agharta, the Subterranean World.

This migration of the Atlantean god-rulers to the Subterranean World, prior to the destruction of Atlantis, was referred to in Teutonic mythology as the "Gotterdamerung" or Twilight of the Gods. They made the journey in flying saucers, which were Atlantean aircraft.

Whereas, in the days of Atlantis, flying saucers flew in the Earth's outer atmosphere, after they entered the Subterranean World they continued to fly in its internal atmosphere in its hollow interior. After the Hiroshima atomic explosion in 1945 they rose again to the surface in numbers, seeking to avert a nuclear catastrophe. The tragedy that befell Atlantis was due to its scientific development running ahead of its moral development, resulting in a nuclear war, which heated the atmosphere, melted polar ice caps and brought on a terrific deluge that submerged the continent. A group of survivors, led by Noah, found refuge in the highlands of Brazil (then an Atlantean colony), where they constructed subterranean cities, connected by tunnels to the surface, to prevent destruction by radioactive fallout and flood.

According to Plato's account, Atlantis was submerged by a series of inundations which came to a climax about 11,500 years ago. Some four million inhabitants lost their lives. Those who were more spiritual and were forewarned escaped in time to Brazil, where, it is claimed, they or their descendants still live in subterranean cities.

In this connection it is interesting to refer to Jules Verne's book, "A Journey To The Center Of The Earth," which presents a similar conception of the earth's formation as did Gardner's book by a similar name. Verne describes a party of explorers who entered a volcanic shaft, and after traveling for months, finally came to the hollow center of the earth, a new world with its own sun to illuminate it, oceans, land and even cities of Atlantean origin. Verne believed that prior to the destruction of Atlantis, some of the Atlanteans escaped and established subterranean cities in the earth's hollow center. Since most of Verne's predictions were later verified, it is possible that this one also will be - but not by entering a volcanic shaft, but by an aerial expedition through the polar openings into the hollow interior of the earth.

One of the early German settlers in Santa Catarina, Brazil, wrote and published a book in old German, dealing with the subterranean world, deriving his information from the Indians. The book described the Earth as being hollow, with a sun in its center. The interior of the earth was said to be inhabited by a disease-free, long-lived race of fruitarians. This subterranean world, the book claimed, was connected by tunnels with the surface, and these tunnels, it was said, opened mostly in Santa Catarina and surrounding parts of South Brazil.

The author has devoted nearly six years to investigations to study the mysterious tunnels which honeycomb Santa Catarina, obviously built by an ancient race to reach subterranean cities. Research is still in progress...

The Russian explorer, Ferdinand Ossendowski, author of "**Beasts, Men and Gods**," claims that the tunnels which encircle the earth and which pass under the Pacific and Atlantic Oceans, were built by men of a pre-glacial Hyperborean civilization which flourished in the polar region at a time when its climate was still tropical, a race of supermen possessing scientific powers of a superior order, and marvelous inventions, including tunnel-boring machines we know nothing about, by means of which they honeycombed the earth with tunnels. We shall now quote from Ossendowski's remarkable book relating his own experiences in Mongolia; where belief in the existence of a subterranean world of Agharta, ruled by the King of the World, who resides in his holy city of Shamballah, is universal. Ossendowski writes:

"'Stop' said my Mongol guide, when we crossed the plateau of Tzagan Luk, 'Stop.'

"His camel bowed down without the need of him ordering it. The Mongol raised his hands in a gesture of adoration and repeated the sacred phrase: *"OM MANI PADME HUM "*

"The other Mongols immediately stopped their camels and began to pray.

SECRET EXPLOITS OF ADMIRAL RICHARD E. BYRD

"'What happened?' I wondered, bringing my camel to a halt.

"The Mongols prayed for some moments, then mounted their camels and rode on.

"'Look;' said the Mongol to me, 'how the camels move their ears with terror, how the manes of the horses remain immobile and alert and how the camels and cattle bow down to the ground. Note how the birds stop flying or the dogs barking. The air vibrates sweetly and one hears a song that penetrates to the hearts of all men, animals and birds. All living beings, seized with fear, prostrate themselves. For the King of the World, in his subterranean palace, is prophesying the future of the peoples of all the earth.'

"Thus spoke the old Mongol.

"Mongolia, with its terrible mountains and limitless plateaus was born a mystery which was preserved by the red and yellow lamas. The rulers of Lhasa and Ourga guarded this science and possessed these mysteries. It was during my trip to Central Asia that I heard for the first time this Mystery of Mysteries, to which I formerly paid no attention, but only did later, when I was able to analyze it and compare certain testimonies frequently subjected to controversy. The old men on the border of Amyil told me an old legend, according to which a Mongolian tribe, seeking to escape from Genghis Khan, hid in a subterranean land. Later, near Nogan Lake, I was shown by Soyota a door which served as the entrance to the kingdom of Agharta.

"It was through this door that a hunter entered into this region and, after he returned told of his visit. The lamas cut off his tongue to prevent him from speaking about the Mystery of Mysteries. In his old age, he returned to the entrance of the cavern and disappeared into the Subterranean World, which memory always brought emotion to the nomad.

"I obtained more detailed information from Houtouktou Jelyl Djamsrap de Narabanch Kure. He told me the history of the arrival of the all-powerful King of the World to the door of exit of the Subterranean World, his appearance, his miracles and prophecies. I then commenced to understand this legend, this hypothesis, this collective vision, which, no matter how we interpret it, conceals not only a mystery but a real force which governs and influences the course of the political life of Asia. From that moment, I commenced my investigations. The lama Gelong, favorite of Prince Choultoun Beyli, gave me a description of the Subterranean World.

"More than six thousand years ago, he said, a holy man disappeared into the earth accompanied by a tribe of people and never returned to its surface. This inner world was also visited by various other men, as Cakya-Muni, Undur-Ghengen Paspa, Baber and others. No one knows where they found the entrance. Some say it was in Afghanistan, others say it was in India.

SECRET EXPLOITS OF ADMIRAL RICHARD E. BYRD

"All inhabitants of this region are protected against evil, and no crime exists within its boundaries. Science developed tranquilly, uninterrupted by war and free from the spirit of destruction. Consequently the subterranean people were able to achieve a much higher degree of wisdom. They compose a vast empire with millions of inhabitants governed by the King of the World. He masters all the forces of nature, can read what is within the souls of all, and in the great book of destiny. Invisibly he rules over eight hundred million human beings, all willing to execute his orders.

"All the subterranean passages in the entire world lead to the World of Agharta. The lamas say that all the subterranean cavities in America are inhabited by this people. The inhabitants of submerged prehistoric continents (Lemuria and Atlantis) found refuge and continued to live in the Subterranean World.

"The lama Turgut, who made the trip from Ourga to Pekin with me, gave me further details: The capital of Agharta (Shamballah) is surrounded by villas where live the Holy Sages. It reminds one of Lhasa, where the temple of the Dalai Lama rises on top of a mountain surrounded by temples and monasteries. His palace is surrounded by the palaces of the Gurus, who control the visible and invisible forces of the earth, from its interior to the sky, and are lords of life and death. If our crazy humanity will continue its wars, they may come to the surface and transform it into a desert. They can dry the oceans, transform continents into seas and cause the disappearance of mountains. In strange vehicles, unknown above, they travel at unbelievable speed through tunnels inside the earth. The lamas found vestiges of these men in all parts and in inscriptions on rocks; and saw remains of the wheels of their vehicles.

"When I asked him to tell me how many persons visited Agharta, the lama answered: `A great number, but most of those who were there maintain the secret as long as they live. When the Olets destroyed Lhasa, one of their regiments, in the mountains of the southwest, reached the limits of Agharta and were then instructed in mysterious sciences, for which reason the Olets and Talmuts became prophets. Certain black tribes of the east also entered Agharta and continued to live there for centuries. Later they were expulsed from the Subterranean World and returned to live on the surface of the earth, bringing with them knowledge of the mystery of prophecy by means of cards and reading the lines of the hand. (They were the ancestors of the gypsies.) In a certain region in the north of Asia there exists a tribe which is on the verge of disappearing and which frequents the caverns of Agharta. Its members can invoke the spirits of dead which live in space.'

"The lama then remained silent some time and then, responding to my thoughts, continued: `In Agharta, the sages write on stone tablets all the sciences of our planet and of other worlds. The Chinese Buddhist sages know that well. Their science is the most advanced and purest. In each century the sages of China

104

united in a secret place near the sea and on the backs of a hundred large turtles that come out of the ocean they write the conclusions of the divine science of their century.'

"This brings to my mind a story that was related to me by an old Chinese attendant in the Temple of Heaven in Pekin. He told me that turtles live for three thousand years without air or food and for this reason all the columns of the blue Temple of Heaven rest on the backs of living turtles, so that wooden supports would not rot.

"Many times did the rulers of Ourga and Lhasa send ambassadors to the King of the World, said the lama librarian, but they could not reach him. However, a Tibetan chief, after a battle with the Olets, came to a cavern whose opening bore the following inscription: "'THIS DOOR LEADS TO AGHARTA.'

"From the cavern left a man of beautiful appearance, who presented to him a Golden tablet bearing strange inscriptions, saying:

"'The King of the World will appear to all men when comes the time of the war of the good against the evil; but this time has not yet come. The worst members of the human race have yet to be born.'

"Chang Chum Ungern sent young Prince Pounzig as an ambassador to the King of the World. The ambassador returned with a letter for the Dalai Lama of Lhasa. He wished to send him a second time but the young ambassador never returned."

CONCLUSION

From the evidence contained in this book, confirmed by many Arctic explorers whom we cite, we come to the following conclusions:

1. There is really no North or South Pole. Where they are supposed to exist there are really wide openings to the hollow interior of the Earth.

2. Flying saucers come from the hollow interior of the Earth through these polar openings.

3. The hollow interior of the earth, warmed by its central sun (the source of Aurora Borealis) has an ideal subtropical climate of about 76 degrees in temperature, neither too hot nor too cold.

4. Arctic explorers found the temperature to rise as they traveled far north; they found more open seas; they found animals traveling north in winter, seeking food and warmth, when they should have gone south; they found the compass needle to assume a vertical position instead of a horizontal one and to become extremely eccentric; they saw tropical birds and more animal life the further north they went; they saw butterflies, mosquitoes and other insects in the extreme north, when they were not found until one is as far south as Alaska and Canada; they found the snow discolored by colored pollen and black dust, which became worse the further north they went. The only explanation is that this dust came from active

volcanoes in the polar opening.

5. There is a large population inhabiting the inner concave surface of the Earth's crust, composing a civilization far in advance of our own in its scientific achievements, which probably descended from the sunken continents of Lemuria and Atlantis. Flying saucers are only one of their many achievements. It would be to our advantage to contact these Elder Brothers of the human race, learn from them and receive their advice and aid.

6. The existence of a polar opening and land beyond the Poles is probably known to the U.S. Navy in whose employ Admiral Byrd made his two historic flights and which is probably a top international secret.

UFO'S OR FLYING SAUCERS IN ANCIENT TIMES
DID SUPER BEINGS FROM SPACE EVER VISIT EARTH?
CLASSICAL WRITERS REPORTED SO

Each Age interprets unusual events in the language of its own experience, whether it be Ezekiel describing sky objects in the symbology of angels and precious jewels, or Monk Lawrence in A.D. 776 marveling at flaming shields from heaven spitting fire at the Saxons besieging Sigiburg, or modern men speculating the Unidentified Flying Objects are of extra-terrestrial origin.

Now that astronomers blazon the belief that life exists throughout the universe, speculation naturally exists that spacemen could have landed on Earth in ages past.

Is there evidence?

For more than 2,000 years it was recorded by nearly all the greatest intellects of Greece and Rome although most of the records of antiquity have been destroyed, in the surviving Classics there is ample evidence of UFO's and probable extra-terrestrial intervention.

Our theologians dismiss the ancient Gods as anthropomorphisms of natural forces, as if entire races for hundreds of years would base their daily lives on lightning and thunderbolts. Yet logic suggests that the old Gods of Egypt, Greece, Rome, Scandinavia and Mexico were not disembodied Spirits or anthropomorphic symbolisms but actual spacemen from the skies. It seems that after the great catastrophes remembered in legends. the "Gods" withdrew and henceforth have been content merely to survey the Earth, except for an occasional intervention in human affairs.

Apollodorus wrote, "Sky was the first who ruled over the whole world," surely signifying domination by space beings. The Roman Emperor Julian vowed, "We must believe that on this world... certain Gods alighted."

Aeschylus, Euripides, Aristophanes, Plautus and Menander frequently introduced a "Deus ex Machine" (a God from a Machine) to untangle the plots of their plays.

Aristotle, Plato, Pliny, Lucretius and most other philosophers believed that the Gods were supermen living in the realms above.

A century ago a German grocer Heinrich Schliemann, using the Iliad as a guide, defied the ridicule of the professors and dug up Troy. Can we dig up records of spaceships in other classics?

Following are some examples from the works of ancient writers, scrutinized for UFO references:

B.C. 498 Visitations "... Castor and Pollux were seen fighting in our army on horseback... Nor do we forget that when the Locrians defeated the people of Crotona in a battle on the banks of the river Sagra, it was known the same day at the Olympian Games. The voices of the Fauns have been heard and deities have appeared in forms so visible that they have compelled everyone who is not senseless or hardened to impiety to confess the presence of the Gods." - Cicero, Of the nature of the Gods, Book I, Ch. 2

B.C. 325: Visitations "There in the stillness of the night both consuls are said to have been visited by the same apparition, a man of greater than human stature, and more majestic, who declared that the commander of one side and the army of the other must be offered up to the Manes and to Mother Earth." - Livy, History, Book VIII, Ch. 11

B.C. 223: Bright Light, Three Moons "At Ariminium a bright light like the day blazed out at night; in many portions of Italy three moons became visible in the night time." - Dio Cassius, Roman History, Book I

B.C. 222: Three Moons "Also three moons have appeared at once, for instance, in the consulship of Gnaeus Domitius and Gaius Fannius." - Pliny, Natural History, Book II, Ch. 32

B.C. 218: The Sky Is Filled "In Amiterno district in many places were seen the appearance of men in white garments from far away. The orb of the sun grew smaller. At Praeneste glowing lamps from heaven. At Arpi a shield in the sky. The moon contended with the sun and during the night two moons were seen. Phantom ships appeared in the sky." - Livy, History, Books XXI-XXII

B.C. 217: Fissure in the Sky "At Faleri the sky had seemed to be rent as it were with a great fissure and through the opening a bright light had shone." - Livy, History, Book XXII, Ch. 1

B.C. 214: Men and Altar "At Hadria an altar was seen in the sky and about it the forms of men in white clothes." - Julius Obsequens, Prodigiorum Libellus, Ch. 66

B.C. 163 : An Extra Sun "In the consulship of Tiberius Gracchus and Manius Juventus at Capua the sun was seen by night. At Formice two suns were seen by day. The sky was afire. In Cephallenia a trumpet seemed to sound from the sky.

There was a rain of earth. A windstorm demolished houses and laid crops flat in the field. By night an apparent sun shone at Pisaurum." - Obsequens, Prodigiorum, Ch 114

B.C. 122: Three Suns, Three Moons "In Gaul three suns and three moons were seen." - Obsequens, Prodigiorum, Ch. 114

B.C. 81: Gold Fireball "Near Spoletium a gold-colored fireball rolled down to the ground, increased in size; seemed to move off the ground toward the east and was big enough to blot out the sun." - Obsequens, Prodigiorum, Ch. 114

B.C. 85: Burning Shield, Sparks "In the consulship of Lucius Valerius and Caius Marius a burning shield scattering sparks ran across the sky. " - Pliny, Natural History, Book II, Ch. 34

B.C. 66: From Spark to Torch "In the consulship of Gnaeus Octavius and Gaius Suetonius a spark was seen to fall from a star and increase in size as it approached the earth. After becoming as large as the moon it diffused a sort of cloudy daylight and then returning to the sky changed into a torch. This is the only record of its occurrence. It was seen by the proconsul Silenus and his suite. " - Pliny, Natural History, Book II, Ch. 35

B.C. 48: Thunderbolts, Visitations "Thunderbolts had fallen upon Pompey's camp. A fire had appeared in the air over Caesar's camp and had fallen upon Pompey's ... In Syria two young men announced the result of the battle (in Thessaly) and vanished." - Dio Cassius, Roman History, Book IV

B.C. 42: Night Light, Three Suns "In Rome light shone so brightly at nightfall that people got up to begin work as though day had dawned. At Murtino three suns were seen about the third hour of the day, which presently drew together in a single orb." - Obsequens, Prodigiorum, Ch. 130

B.C.?: Suns, Moons, Globes "How often has our Senate enjoined the decemvirs to consult the books of the Sibyl: For instance, when two suns had been seen or when three moons had appeared and when flames of fire were noticed in the sky; or on that other occasion when the sun was beheld in the night, when noises were heard in the sky, and the heaven itself seemed to burst open, and strange globes were remarked in it." - Cicero, On Divination, Book I, Ch. 43

A.D. 70: Chariots in the Sky "On the 21st of May a demonic phantom of incredible size... For before sunset there appeared in the air over the whole country chariots and armed troops coursing through the clouds and surrounding the cities." - Josephus, Jewish War, Book CXI

A.D. 193: Three New Stars "Three stars ... suddenly came into view surrounding the sun, when Emperor Julianus in our presence was offering the Sacrifice of Entrance in front of the Senate House. These stars were so very distinct that the soldiers kept continually looking at them and pointing them out to another . . . " - Dio Cassius, Roman History, Book LXXIV

SECRET EXPLOITS OF ADMIRAL RICHARD E. BYRD

A.D. 217: Visitation "In Rome, moreover, a 'Spirit' having the appearance of a man led an ass up to the Capitol and afterward to the palace seeking its master as he claimed and stating that Antoninus was dead and Jupiter was now Emperor. Upon being arrested for this and sent by Matermainus to Antoninus he said, 'I go as you bid but I shall face not this emperor but another.' And when he reached Capua he vanished. " - Dio Cassius, Roman History

The above references are only a sampling of the evidence available. Consider just four writers: Julius Obsequens recorded 63 celestial phenomena; Livy, 30; Pliny, 26; Dio Cassius, 14; Cicero, 9.

Romans fervently believed that two strange horsemen, taller than normal men, alike in age, height and beauty, saved the day for Posthumus at Lake Regillus and, that same day, miraculously appeared in the Forum, announced the victory, and departed forever.

A contemporary historian described two shiny shields spitting fire around the rims, diving repeatedly at the columns of Alexander the Great in India, stamping horses and elephants, and then returning to the sky.

When we recall that Romulus was borne to heaven by a whirlwind while giving judgment on the Palatine Hill, that his successor Numa Pomilius, used magic weapons, that Livy, Pliny the Elder, and Julius Obsequens tell of mysterious voices, celestial trumpets, men in white garments hovering in airships, several suns and moons together, sudden new stars, and superhuman apparitions descending among men and then vanishing, we suddenly feel we are reading the wonders of the Bible.

By some strange twist of the human mind, we worship prodigies in old Palestine as manifestations of the Lord, yet scoff at identical phenomena occurring at the same time only a few hundred miles away.

Evidence exists; all we need to do is examine it.

Note: As Dr. Bernard reveals there are many cities beneath our feet – in the following chapters we visit but a few! - TGB

10

AGHARTA: LAND OF ENCHANTMENT
By Sean Casteel

(Since there are a few variations on the spelling of Agharta, we made the editorial decision to simply use whatever spelling was used in the original source's material. It is perhaps an interesting irony that there is no consensus on how to spell a word that typically means "paradise.")

Belief in the Hollow Earth has many adherents in our time, but the idea had its beginnings in times long ago. Among the wealth of available material on the ancient mystery is an article by Dr. Joshua David Stone called "Aghartha In The Hollow Earth!" in which he explains why he has crossed over into the believer's camp.

"The biggest cover-up of all time," Stone writes, "conceals the fact that there is a civilization living in the center of the Earth known as 'Aghartha.' This may be hard for some of you to believe. I know it was for me at first. However, I now have an absolute knowingness of the truth of this."

Stone begins by referring to a fervent belief in Aghartha in Buddhist theology.

"They believe it to be of a race of supermen and women," he explains, "who occasionally come to the surface to oversee the development of the human race. They also believe that this subterranean world has millions of inhabitants and many cities and that their capital is called 'Shamballa.' The Master of this world was believed to have given orders to the Dalai Lama of Tibet, who was his terrestrial representative. His messages were being transmitted through certain secret tunnels that connect this Inner World with Tibet."

Stone also draws on the testimony of Nicholas Roerich, a famous Russian channel for the Ascended Master El Morya, who claimed that Lhasa, the capital of Tibet, was connected by a tunnel with Shamaballa. The tunnel's entrance was guarded by lamas who were sworn to secrecy. Another tunnel was believed to connect the secret chambers at the base of the Great Pyramid in Giza with Aghartha.

A similar belief is held by the Hindus of India and is recorded in one of their

SECRET EXPLOITS OF ADMIRAL RICHARD E. BYRD

most fundamental religious texts, the Ramayana, which tells the story of the great Avatar Rama. The Ramayana describes Rama as an "emissary from Aghartha" who arrived in an air vehicle. Stone believes it is "quite extraordinary" that both the Buddhist and Hindu religions independently refer to Aghartha and cites this as evidence for its reality.

From some basic ancient references to the Hollow Earth, Stone moves on to the story of Rear Admiral Richard Byrd's 1947 flight over the North Pole, a story those reading this book will find familiar. Stone draws on Byrd's "secret diary" as his primary source and relates how the veteran Navy pilot entered the Hollow Earth and traveled 1,700 miles over mountains, lakes, rivers, with abundant green vegetation and animal life. Byrd would also find cities and a thriving civilization.

"His plane was finally greeted by flying machines of a type he had never seen before," Stone writes. "They escorted him to a safe landing place, and he was graciously greeted by emissaries from Aghartha."

The beings told Byrd that he had been allowed to enter Aghartha because of his high moral and ethical character. They said that in the aftermath of the atomic bombing of Hiroshima and Nagasaki they had become concerned about their own safety and survival. The beings said they now felt compelled to make a more open contact with the outside world to ensure that we did not destroy our own world and their civilization along with it. It was for this reason Byrd had been chosen for contact, a person they felt could be trusted.

Byrd and his crew were then guided by their hosts back to the outer world. In January 1956, Byrd led another expedition to the South Pole, during which he and his crew penetrated for 2,300 miles into the center of the Earth. Byrd also testified to the fact that the Inner Earth is lit by its own sun and reasoned that the poles of the Earth are convex rather than concave, which thus allows ships and planes to enter freely.

It is here that Stone reports on the alleged cover-up.

"The American press announced Byrd's discovery," he writes. "However, it was immediately suppressed by our good friends, the Secret Government. Ray Palmer, the editor of 'Flying Saucer Magazine,' did a detailed story on Byrd's discoveries. The U.S. government either bought, stole or destroyed almost every copy and then even destroyed the plates at the printing press."

When "The National Geographic" released an article on Byrd's adventure, the U.S. government again intervened and "gobbled up" every issue, according to Stone. But further confirmation of Byrd's suppressed claims is found in a book by Dr. Raymond Bernard called "The Hollow Earth." In Bernard's oft-cited tome, a Los Angeles doctor named Nephi Cotton reported that one of his patients told him the following story:

"I lived near the Arctic Circle in Norway," the patient begins. "One sum-

Inspirational artist Carol Ann Rodriguez envisions a serenely beautiful underground kingdom for those living in such places as Agharta and Telos beneath Mount Shasta.

Even independent film makers are adapting the magic of such mystical Inner Earth cities as Agharta to their storylines, as witness this forthcoming motion picture.

"They spoke to us in a strange language!"

"There must have been five hundred of these thunder-throated monsters!"

Willis George Emerson's father, Olaf Jansen, told of a journey by outrigger to an opening in the ice where he met a race of giants as well as woolly mastodons who have been thought to have been extinct for thousands of years.

The late Dr. Joshua David Stone invisioned Agharta as being populated by a race of masterful beings.

"Agharta" is a 1975 live double album by American jazz trumpeter, composer and bandleader Miles Davis. At the record label's suggestion, it was titled after the legendary subterranean city Agharta. Davis enlisted Japanese artist Tadanori Yokoo to design its artwork, which depicted the cityscape of an advanced civilization with elements inspired by Eastern subterranean myths and Afro futurism.

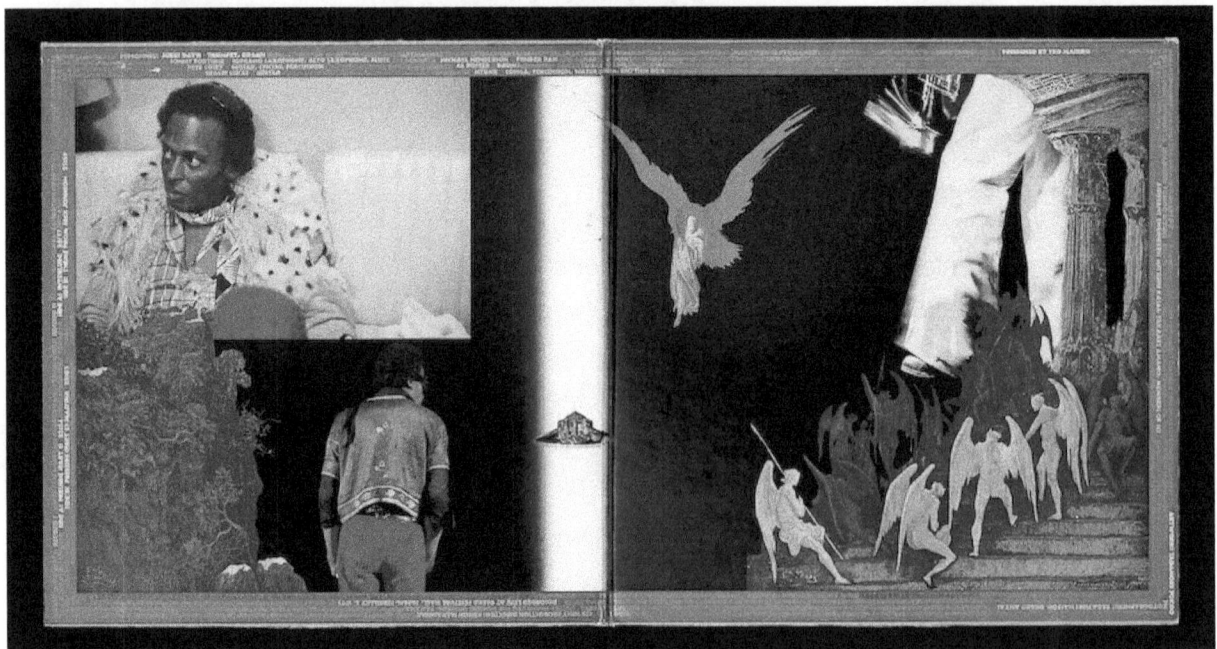

THE LONG LOST BOOKS
OF RAMPA FEATURING. . .

MY VISIT
TO AGHARTA

T. LOBSANG
RAMPA

om mani padme hum

The SMOKY GOD
And Other Inner Earth Mysteries
Updated / Expanded Edition

Edited by Timothy Green Beckley

Additional Material by Commander X,
Scott Corrales, Dennis Crenshaw,
Brad Steiger, Tim Swartz and Sean Casteel

Dordjelutru Lamasery

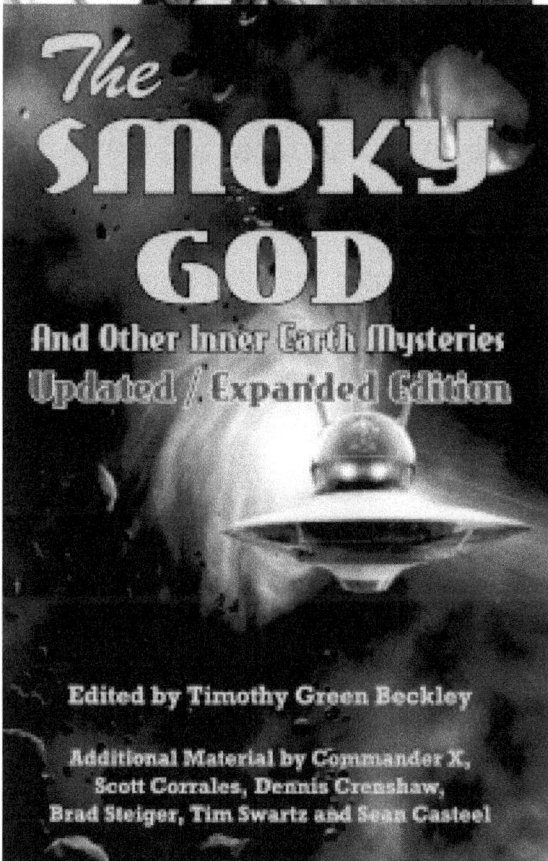

Sangma RED LAMA. Messenger of Buddha
(Robert Ernst Dickhoff and his son Robert, Jr.)

Popular authors like T. Lobsang Rampa have added in recent years to the body of works on the Buddhist concept of the lost land of Agharta.

Journeyman Nicholas Roerich saw a UFO while high in the mountains surrounding Tibet, where he claimed a lost underground city was located. He was at least partially responsible for getting the eye in the center of the pyramid placed on the back of the U.S. dollar.

Buddhist Robert Dickhoff, seen in his rather cluttered NYC apartment, incorporated Agharta as part of his cultural doctrine as early as the late 1940s.

Though many editions of The Smoky God are available, this volume by Inner Light - Global Communications is by far the most complete.

mer my friend and I made up our minds to take a boat trip together and go as far as we could into the North Country. So we put a month's worth of food provisions in a small fishing boat and set to sea. At the end of one month, we had traveled far into the north, beyond the pole and into a strange new country. We were much astonished by the weather there."

The temperature was so warm that even at night it was difficult to sleep. One day they saw a mountain into which the ocean seemed to be emptying. Mystified, they stayed their course and found themselves sailing into a vast canyon that led into the interior of the Earth. They soon saw the same sun shining within the Earth that has been reported down through the ages. The ocean he and his friend were traveling on gradually became a river, a river that connects the inner surface of the world from one end to the other.

"It can take you, if you follow it long enough, from the North Pole through to the South Pole," Dr. Cotton's Nordic patient claimed.

The anonymous storyteller continued by saying, "We saw that the inner surface of the Earth was divided, as the other one is, into both land and water. There is plenty of sunshine. We sailed further and further into this fantastic country – fantastic because everything was huge in size as compared with things on the outside. Plants are big, trees gigantic. Finally we came upon giants. They were dwelling in homes and towns, just as we do on the Earth's surface, and they used a type of electrical conveyance, like a monorail car, to transport people. It ran along the river's edge from town to town."

The two Nordic gentlemen were soon spotted by some of the giants dwelling in this Inner Earth paradise. The giants seemed amazed at seeing the two normal-sized travelers but kindly offered food and lodging to the pair of interlopers. The Nordic pair stayed with the giants for one year and observed many strange and wonderful things. They were continually amazed at the underground dwellers' scientific progress and high-tech inventions.

"All of this time they were never unfriendly to us," the doctor records the patient as saying. "We were allowed to return home in the same manner in which we came. In fact, they courteously offered their protection if we should need it for the return voyage."

A SECRET TREATY WITH THE HOLLOW EARTH

Has the U.S. entered into a treaty with the denizens of the Hollow Earth? We can at least say it is an idea getting some attention on the Internet. The story starts with the arrest of a spy in Germany.

"A truly bizarre Federal Security Service (FSB) report circulating in the Kremlin today on the Foreign Intelligence Service (SVR) 'asset' arrested yesterday by Germany's National Intelligence Service (BND) for spying states that this German national has provided to Russian officials 'compelling evidence' that the United

SECRET EXPLOITS OF ADMIRAL RICHARD E. BYRD

States has entered into a 'secret pact' with 'unnamed forces' inhabiting our Earth's interior regions for the purpose of ruling the world."

The man arrested was identified by Western media sources only as Manfred K., age 60, who stated that he intended to give the information to a "third party," which unconfirmed reports say was the SVR. Manfred K. was a civilian worker at the U.S.-NATO Ramstein Air Base located in the German state of Rheinland-Pfalz, which is the command and control hub for the Western alliance's European missile defense forces and headquarters of the U.S. Air Force in Europe. In his work there, Manfred K. had access to many classified documents.

Some of the intelligence Manfred K. turned over to the Russians included maps produced by the German Nazi regime in the 1930s and 1940s detailing their underground bases located in Antarctica as well as – most shockingly – our Earth's hollow interior and the lands that exist there.

It is important to note that Germany has long been fascinated with Antarctica after prominent German scientist Johann Carl Friedrich Gauss (1777-1855), who is ranked as one of history's most influential mathematicians, stated that all of Earth's history, physics and geography could only be explained by our planet having a hollow, and populated, interior with entrances being located at both the North and South Poles. From 1901 to 1903 Germany conducted its first exploration of Antarctica in what is called the Gauss Expedition where they claimed for themselves vast areas of our planet's southernmost continent.

The great American explorer, Admiral Robert Edwin Peary, Sr., was fascinated by the discoveries made by German scientists during the Gauss Expedition and embarked on a similar mission. In 1909, Peary became the first man to reach the North Pole and was awarded the Imperial German Geographical Society Nachtigall gold medal, among many other international awards and honors.

With many questions about the true nature of the poles still unanswered, in 1938 Chancellor Adolph Hitler ordered another expedition to Antarctica that lasted until the following year. What was discovered in Antarctica by the Nazis to this day remains highly classified among all the top world governments, with many speculating that a "deal" to end World War II was made between Germany and the U.S. that allowed the Americans to gain German technology – including atomic bombs, missile technology, jetfighter technology, etc. – in exchange for allowing top Nazi leaders (including Hitler) to "retreat" to the massive bases they had built in and under the Southern Continent.

The following theory about "Operation High Jump" is also worth examining.

In 1946 the Western Allies, led by the U.S., apparently decided to retake Antarctica from the Nazis in what was called "Operation High Jump." Though this mission was purported to be for scientific reasons, numerous other reports state that these American-led forces were forced to retreat after having lost over 1,500 troops and suffering massive military material losses. Returning in 1947 to the U.S., Admiral Richard E. Byrd, the commander of Operation High Jump, is said to have warned that the largest menace came now from the South Pole, because they had observed airships there that could fly to impressive speeds.

One should further note the remarks made by Hollow Earth researcher Dr. R.W. Bernard, who, in his 1964 book titled "The Hollow Earth: The Greatest Geographical Discovery in History," credited Byrd with discovering both the North and South Pole openings to the inner reaches of our planet.

"To the future explorers of the New World that exists beyond the North and South Poles in the hollow interior of the Earth," Bernard writes in his dedication, "who will repeat Admiral Byrd's historic flight for 1,700 miles beyond the North Pole and that of his expedition for 2,300 miles beyond the South Pole, entering a new, unknown territory not shown on any map, covering an immense land area whose total size is larger than North America, consisting of forests, mountains, lakes, vegetation and animal life. The aviator who will be the first to reach this New Territory, unknown until Admiral Byrd first discovered it, will go down in history as a New Columbus. And greater than Columbus, for while Columbus discovered a new continent, he will discover a New World."

If this FSB report can be taken at face value, and the U.S. has entered into an agreement   with those who inhabit our Inner Earth, it behooves us to acknowledge that the ancient symbol associated with these Inner Earth peoples is an ancient one, dating back to the very beginning of time from the ancient Indus Valley Civilization, but more well-known for its last incarnation as being the hated and feared symbol used by the Nazi Germans called the swastika.

Western governments and their intelligence services actively campaign against the information found in these reports so as not to alarm their citizens about the many catastrophic Earth changes and events to come, a stance that many believers strongly disagree with. We believe that it is every human being's right to know the truth.

THE COLD HARD FACTS: THE "STRAIGHT MEDIA"
REPORTS ON ANTARCTIC MYSTERIES

The mystery surrounding Antarctica sometimes receives notice even from the "straight media." Even nonbelievers are forced at times to examine the evidence and report on tantalizing bits of info that would seem to reinforce the notion that there is more lurking beneath the surface at the South Pole than is acknowledged by mainstream science.

For example, in December 2016, a U.K. newspaper called The Daily Mail ran with a news item under the following headline: "Is there a Nazi UFO site buried in the Antarctic?"

SECRET EXPLOITS OF ADMIRAL RICHARD E. BYRD

"A bizarre new theory suggests that a mysterious anomaly discovered in the Antarctic may hide a Nazi UFO base," writes reporter Harry Pettit. "The theory comes from a team of UFO hunters who claim that the Nazis built secret bases in Antarctica during World War II that were designed to be used by UFOs."

According to a report by Jasper Hamill, writing in the U.K. newspaper, The Sun, "Scientists believe a massive object which could change our understanding of history is hidden beneath the Antarctic ice. The huge and mysterious 'anomaly' is thought to be lurking beneath the frozen wastes of an area called Wilkes Land. It stretches for a distance of 151 miles across and has a maximum depth of about 848 meters. Some researchers believe it is the remains of a truly massive asteroid which was more than twice the size of the Chicxulub space rock that wiped out the dinosaurs."

This "Wilkes Land gravity anomaly" was first uncovered in 2006, when NASA satellites spotted gravitational changes which indicated the presence of a huge object sitting in the middle of a 300 mile wide impact crater.

The UFO hunters promoting what The Daily Mail called a "bizarre theory" go by the name Secure Team 10 and have posted several UFO-related videos on YouTube. Part of the narration for their video about the Wilkes Land anomaly declares: "To this day, scientists have no idea or any way to discover exactly what is buried deep under this thick ice-shelf. This continent has been shrouded in a mystery of its own for years now."

Secure Team 10 suggested that the Nazis built secret bases in Antarctica during World War II that were designed to be used by flying saucers, adding that "There is some evidence of this coming to light in recent years, such as images purporting to show various entrances built into the side of mountains with a saucer shape and at a very high altitude. This begs the question, how could you enter these entrances without something that could fly and was the same shape as the hole itself?"

The straight media even acknowledges conspiracy theories about Operation High Jump.

"The conspiracy theorists also discuss the possibility that the U.S. Navy led a mission to investigate the mysterious anomaly," writes Pettit. "They claim that the mission was dubbed 'Operation High Jump,' which some conspiracy theorists think was an attempt to find the entrance to a hidden world beneath Earth.

"This is not the first time that a strange UFO conspiracy has arisen from Antarctica's icy depths," he continues. "Earlier this year, a strange theory claiming that there is a mysterious pyramid in the Antarctic emerged. Conspiracy theorists posted a video on YouTube in which they claimed that U.S. Secretary of State

SECRET EXPLOITS OF ADMIRAL RICHARD E. BYRD

John Kerry visited Antarctica in November 2016 to visit an 'alien base' within the pyramid. The video suggested that the images had been taken from Google Earth, but it is unclear whether they had been edited. The video was posted by Third Phase of the Moon, another YouTube channel that regularly posts conspiracy theories on aliens."

[A cautionary note from Tim Beckley: Readers should be alerted to the fact that Third Phase of the Moon has a reputation for posting "fake news" along with what might be fairly legitimate stories.]

The straight press, for all their claims to objectivity and dedication to the "cold, hard facts," does at least manage to grant a modicum of dignity to conspiracy theorists and UFO believers, although journalists ceaselessly qualify themselves by the use of adjectives like "bizarre" and "strange." Perhaps one day the truth about Antarctica, Operation High Jump, secret Nazi bases, etc., will itself become mainstream and be taught as part of the standard history curriculum in our schools. In the meantime, there are occasional moments where the fringe and the mainstream intersect, as in the case of the Wilkes Land anomaly.

UFOS: DO SOME OF THEM COME FROM
AN INNER EARTH "PARADISE?"

Do UFOs, or flying saucers, originate from an Inner Earth Paradise? That may sound like it's kind of a stretch, but a selection of books from Tim Beckley's Global Communications and Inner Light Publications make the argument that they most certainly do, eschewing any beliefs that the mysterious visitors come from outer space at all.

The most recent offering to make the case for the Inner Earth Paradise is called "The Smoky God and Other Inner Earth Mysteries," and includes a reprint of a book written by a Norwegian fisherman named Olaf Jansen. Jansen claims to have journeyed by boat with his father to a lush and peaceful land occupied by a race of kindly giants.

"My father," Jansen writes, "was an ardent believer in Odin and Thor, and had frequently told me they were gods who came from far beyond the 'North Wind.' There was a tradition, my father explained, that still farther northward was a land more beautiful than any that mortal man had ever known, and that it was inhabited by the 'Chosen.'"

One day, as father and son decide to try to actually travel to this land of the "Chosen," and take a detour from their fishing trip to sail due north. Instead of a forbidding, frozen wasteland, they find the land of the "Smoky God," a place hidden inside the hollow Earth.

Jansen's book is introduced by an American writer named Willis George Emerson, who befriended Jansen in the old Norseman's last days, which were spent rather idyllically in a bungalow in Los Angeles. According to Emerson, "Take an eggshell, and from each end break out a piece as large as the end of a pencil. Extract its contents, and then you will have a perfect representation of Olaf Jansen's Earth. The distance from the inside surface to the outside surface, according to him, is about three hundred miles."

Jansen also provides us with another analogy. A man builds a house for himself and his family. The porches or verandas are all without and are secondary. The building is really constructed for the conveniences within. In like manner, God created the Earth for the sake of that which is "within," and thus Jansen's claim to have discovered the original Garden of Eden INSIDE the Earth, still flourishing and still the same kind of paradise described in the Book of Genesis.

But Jansen's miraculous discovery did not come without a price. He informs the reader that, "I dare not allow the facts as I know them to be published while I am living, for fear of further humiliation, confinement and suffering. First of all, I was put in irons by the captain of the whaling vessel that rescued me, for no other reason than that I told the truth about the marvelous discoveries made by my father and myself. But this was far from being the end of my tortures."

Jansen next made the mistake of telling his uncle what had happened, even asking his prosperous uncle to finance another trip north to the hidden paradise. His uncle at first appeared interested and sympathetic, and urged Jansen to repeat his story to certain government officials.

"Imagine my disappointment and horror," Jansen writes, "when, upon the conclusion of my narrative, certain papers were signed by my uncle, and, without warning, I found myself arrested and hurried away to dismal and fearful confinement in a madhouse, where I remained for twenty-eight years – long, tedious, frightful years of suffering!"

After his release, Jansen returned to fishing, eventually making enough money to start his own fishing business. He then sold his business and moved to America, ending up in Los Angeles and passing along his manuscript to the sympathetic Emerson as he lay on his deathbed. The rediscovery of Eden, it seems, was no picnic for Jansen.

Jansen's story, first published in 1908, while sad, does help to sketch in the boundaries of the hollow or Inner Earth, and from there a selection of more current writers pick up the ball and run with it. For example, an article by the late Ray Palmer, the legendary pioneer of 20th century paranormal journalism, lays out Palmer's rationale for why the flying saucers most likely do not come from outer space.

At the time Palmer's article was written, in 1959, he was the editor of a pulp magazine called "Flying Saucers."

"'Flying Saucers' has amassed a large file of evidence," Palmer writes, "which its editors consider unassailable, to prove that the flying saucers are native to the planet Earth; that the governments of more than one nation (if not all of them) know this to be a fact; that a concerted effort is being made to learn all about them, and to explore their native land; that the facts already known are considered so important that they are the world's top secret; that the danger is so great that to offer public proof is to risk widespread panic; that public knowledge would bring public demand for action which would topple governments both helpless and unwilling to comply; that the inherent nature of the flying saucers and their origination area is completely disruptive to the political and economic status quo."

For most people reading this article, that much is already a given. But Palmer argues further that one is mistaken in assuming that Kenneth Arnold's 1947 sighting is the real "day one" of flying saucers, and that the phenomenon has been with us since ancient times and even before. Since the saucers have been with us from the very beginning, how can we say they originated elsewhere, from somewhere a vast distance away from Earth? Yet in spite of their earthly origin, the secrecy is still strictly enforced, which has led to countless conspiracy theories and rumors of governmental/alien collusion that will most likely persist until the truth is publicly revealed.

It is just such a cover-up of earthly UFOs that Admiral Richard E. Byrd comes up against in another Global Communications book called "The Secret Lost Diary of Admiral Richard E. Byrd and the Phantom of the Poles." The book begins with an introductory chapter by Michael X, which lays a foundation for what follows with this strange story about Admiral Byrd.

"In the year 1947," Michael X writes, "Admiral Richard E. Byrd made a flight into the South Polar region of the world. Before he started on the venture, Byrd made a mysterious statement: 'I'd like to see that land beyond the Pole. That area beyond the Pole in the center of the great unknown.' In the cockpit of his plane was a powerful two-way radio. When Byrd and his scientific companions took off from their base at the South Pole, they managed to fly 1700 miles beyond it. That's when the radio in Byrd's plane was put into use to report something utterly incredible."

According to Byrd's radio transmission, there was a strange, great valley beneath them. For some unknown reason, the valley Byrd saw was not ice-covered, as it should have been in the frigid Antarctic.

"It was green and luxuriant," Michael X goes on. "There were mountains with thick forests of trees on them. There was lush grass and underbrush."

The temperature was a balmy 75 degrees.

"Suddenly, the press and radio were 'hushed up.' After the first brief messages leaked through to the newspapers, no further confirmation of the big discovery was given. Was it merely a hoax? Some newsman's joke? I think not."

SECRET EXPLOITS OF ADMIRAL RICHARD E. BYRD

Michael X believes instead that Byrd had come upon a great doorway or entrance leading deep into the unknown interior of the Earth. This is of course reminiscent of Olaf Jansen's eggshell analogy, which posits openings at both the North and South Poles leading into the Inner Earth Paradise.

But the book goes even further, offering what is purported to be Admiral Byrd's own secret diary made during an even stranger journey to the North Pole.

"I must write this diary in secrecy and obscurity," Byrd begins. "It concerns my Arctic flight of the nineteenth day of February in the year of Nineteen and Forty Seven. There comes a time when the rationality of men must fade into insignificance and one must accept the inevitability of the Truth! I am not at liberty to disclose the following documentation at this writing. Perhaps it shall never see the light of public scrutiny, but I must do my duty and record here for all to read one day."

The Flight Log begins with standard notes about the plane ride itself, such as discovering the fuel mixture on the starboard engine being too rich. Another entry confirms that the radio is working correctly, while still another complains of encountering slight turbulence which then abates. At 0915 hours, Byrd sights a small mountain range in the distance. After another 29 minutes, he confirms that the mountains are still visible and are no illusion. By 1000 hours, they are crossing the mountain range and see a valley with a small river or stream running through it.

"There should be no green valley below," he writes. "Something is definitely wrong and abnormal here! We should be over ice and snow! To the portside are great forests growing on the mountain slopes. Our navigation instruments are still spinning, the gyroscope is oscillating back and forth!"

Byrd continues to see more rolling green hills and remarks that the temperature is now 74 degrees. Meanwhile, the radio has stopped functioning. Next he sees what appears to be a city, which he says is impossible. Then, on both sides of Byrd's plane, a strange type of aircraft is coming rapidly alongside.

"They are disc-shaped and have a radiant quality to them," he writes. "They are close enough now to see the markings on them. It is a type of Swastika!!! This is fantastic. Where are we? What has happened?"

After about five more minutes, Byrd hears a voice crackling on the radio, speaking with a slight Nordic or Germanic accent and saying, "Welcome, Admiral, to our domain. We shall land you in exactly seven minutes. Relax, Admiral, you are in good hands." The engines of Byrd's plane have ceased to function and the aircraft is now flying by some strange unknown method, its controls now useless. It begins to descend as though caught in an elevator and lands gently. Several tall, blond men approach, and there is a large shimmering city in the distance that pulsates with the colors of the rainbow. It is there that Byrd's logbook entries end, and he says he tells the rest of the story from memory.

SECRET EXPLOITS OF ADMIRAL RICHARD E. BYRD

"It defies the imagination," he says as the log portion of his writings concludes, "and would seem all but madness if it had not happened."

Perhaps it is better at this point to save the rest of the story for those who actually read the book and thus avoid the kind of spoilers that would sap the tale of its strength as it builds to a climax of high strangeness – with the kind of bizarre revelations that Byrd was probably wise to keep to himself. Who are the blond strangers in the disc-shaped craft? What is the brightly colored city seen in the background? What message do these kindly abductors deliver to Byrd and eventually to us?

The truths we finally learn are so completely unbelievable that there is no need to question why Byrd hesitates to reveal them publicly, no doubt fearing the same fate as befell Olaf Jansen, to be locked away in a madhouse, protesting the fact of his sanity to deaf ears.

The same volume also includes the complete text of "The Phantom of the Poles," written by William Reed and first published in 1906. Reed has his own adventures in the Polar Regions and labors mightily to convince the reader that the Earth is hollow and that there are entrances to the Inner Earth at both the North and South Poles. Sometimes the science he uses to make his arguments is quite naturally a little dated, but for those interested in the Inner Earth phenomenon, his book is an essential historical document.

T. LOBSANG RAMPA ENTERS AGHARTA

But there is still another voice demanding to be heard in the story of an Inner Earth Paradise. Before his death in 1981, occult scholar and metaphysical philosopher T. Lobsang Rampa acquired a small – but nevertheless dedicated – following. In his lifetime, Rampa wrote over a dozen books designed to help seekers looking for a certain kind of truth discover for themselves the secrets of existence as filtered through his intimate knowledge of the astral plane and other otherworldly dimensions. While the main body of his work has been out of print for the last several years, Inner Light Publications has recently begun to publish reprints of Rampa's books for a new audience eager to learn from a proven master just how this universe functions on a metaphysical level.

Rampa books reprinted by Tim Beckley's publishing enterprise includes "Candlelight," "The Hermit," "Tibetan Sage," "My Visit To Venus," "Beyond The Tenth," "Cave of The Ancients," "Chapters Of Life," "The Saffron Robe," as well as a special meditation and prayer tape Rampa recorded back in the 1960s, and a book called "Living With The Lama," telepathically communicated by the writer's pet cat who describes what it's like living with the Lama. The books are obtainable from Amazon or from the publisher directly.

While not his main subject of discourse, Rampa certainly penned thousands of words about his venturing into a vast cavern system beneath the Tibetan city of

Lhasa. He seemed to hold a cherished belief in the existence of the Inner Earth and gave the following reasons for his personal belief that our planet is hollow:

1. Commercial airlines do not actually fly over the poles, as the navigational instruments would go awry.

2. No one has ever really been to the poles, only near them.

3. There is an atomic sun in the center of the Earth which is responsible for the auroras.

4. The current model of geophysics (crust/mantle/core) is not based upon any solid evidence, merely supposition.

5. The Inner Earth is about 2.9 times bigger than the Moon. This makes it actually larger than the land area on the outside of the Earth.

6. Inner World-ers are remnants of Lemuria/Mu/Atlantis and even older civilizations who escaped from surface cataclysms by entering the cavern system.

7. There is a legend that the gypsies are descendants from Inner-Worlders.

8. The government denies the existence of the hollow Earth in order to avoid a panic.

9. Certain UFOs come from the inner world.

10. Photographs of the Polar Regions do not show holes, only shadows and patches.

LHASA – THE SUBTERRANEAN CITY BENEATH TIBET

Rampa himself told of visiting several subterranean worlds. The author of "Rampa, New Age Trailblazer," Karen Mutten, reminds us of his words on this very subject taken from "Doctor From Lhasa" and the earlier "My Visit To Venus," a privately issued tome which Rampa later claimed should not have been circulated for a variety of reasons, the main one being that, while his accounts were true, they would be difficult for some of his readers to understand or accept.

The opening chapter, "Home of the Gods," continues on from "Doctor From Lhasa's" description of a visit to the Chang Tang Highlands, where the lamas discovered a huge, ancient city. Half frozen in a glacier, this city had once accommodated a race of giants.

"We took flaring torches," Rampa writes, "and cautiously climbed down what seemed to be endless steps and slithered along smooth rocky passages. These tunnels, I was told, had been made by volcanic action countless centuries before. On the walls were strange diagrams and drawings of quite unfamiliar scenes. I was more interested in seeing the lake which I had been told stretched for miles and miles at the end of one passage.

"At last we entered a tunnel," Rampa continues, "which grew wider and wider, until suddenly the roof disappeared to where the light of our torches would not reach. A hundred yards more, and we stood at the edge of water such as I had never seen before. It was black and still, with the blackness that made it appear almost invisible, more like a bottomless pit than a lake."

Rampa saw several extraordinary sights in this underground chamber he couldn't possibly explain. On the cave walls he noticed numerous unknown figures, strange, geometric shapes and images of giants. There were also depictions of alien machines along with cryptic stones. Had he just entered Lhasa? What was the meaning of this hidden chamber beneath the Earth?

Returning to Rampa's narrative: "Nearby in a spacious courtyard, there was an immense metal structure which reminded me of two of our temple dishes clamped together and was clearly a vehicle of some sort."

The monks cautiously approached the vehicle, which was about 50 to 60 feet (15.24 to 18.29 meters) across, and ascended a ladder leading inside. Once inside, Rampa's Guide touched something which caused the ship to hum and emit a bluish light. To their surprise, they were approached by large humans who communicated telepathically:

"Be not afraid, for we were aware of your coming for the past hundred years. We made provisions so that those who were intrepid enough to enter this vessel should know the past."

The humanoids showed them pictures from the past civilization: huge buildings which sat by the sea with disc-like vehicles soaring above. They witnessed an enormous explosion which toppled the buildings and caused a tsunami to rise above the ruins.

The humanoids told them of a "White Brotherhood," composed of incarnate and discarnate entities, which safeguarded all life.

The chapter continued with the seven lamas being taken up into space from where they could see Tibet. The vehicle left the atmosphere, with no increase in gravity or sensation of speed, and soared into space. The monks were taken on a tour of the spaceship. Its propulsion system utilized a form of magnetism which repelled the Earth's magnetism. The repelling force could be adjusted to allow the vessel to hover, rise or sink. The ship was also capable of collecting "space electricity" – a form of magnetism based upon cosmic energy.

The Venusian hosts took the lamas in a strange vehicle to the Hall of Knowledge, where they observed the Earth's creation along with the mighty civilizations of Lemuria, Atlantis and Poseidonia.

The Broad One warned: "We guard the Earth, for, if man's folly is allowed to go unchecked, terrible things will happen to the race of man. There are powers upon the Earth, human powers who oppose all thoughts of our ships, who say there is nothing greater than the human upon Earth, so there cannot be ships from other worlds."

Eventually, after many days, the Tibetans were returned to Earth, "which now seemed a tawdry place" and "paled into insignificance against the glory of Venus." The story ended with this:

"Never again, I thought, shall I see such wonderful things. How mistaken I was, for that was but the first of many trips."

Rampa's "My Visit To Agharta" includes previously unpublished material taken from manuscripts found in the personal effects of a bookseller in New York who befriended Rampa and published some of his earlier work. The book takes its title from its first section, in which Rampa tells an incredible yet curiously believable story about a journey to the Inner Earth, accompanied by a Tibetan lama named Mingyar Dondup. Along the way, they manage to rescue a young woman who has been kidnapped and tortured by demonic dwellers in the underground tunnels that lead to Agharta. The woman's fate is not unique, we are told. Thousands disappear that way every year, making up the statistics of missing persons who are never heard from again.

But the real purpose of the sojourn into the depths below is to reach Agharta itself, which turns out to be a garden paradise at the center of the Earth as well as at the center of every other habitable planet in the universe simultaneously. There Rampa and his friend the lama take part in a kind of convention of wise men and saints, both human and alien, and witness a demonstration of the power of the light that sustains life throughout eternity. This sun-like body in Rampa's Agharta is the same as Olaf Jansen's "Smoky God," a reference to the slightly dimmed orb to which the underground dwellers offer worship and praise.

In a section of the book called "Ancient Aircraft of the Gods," Rampa writes about the highly advanced flying machines of India as described in the ancient text called "Mahabharata," ships that flew on "an enormous ray which was as brilliant as the sun and made a noise like the thunder of a storm." Rampa says the ships used to shoot up and down the tunnels that connected the inner and surface worlds, but they now lay mostly unused except for occasional trips through hidden exits to the surface.

"Like the flying saucer sightings above ground," Rampa laments, "the tunnel sightings are mostly considered folklore. Nevertheless, it would not surprise me if the deepest recesses of the planet still hold those who know how to use the ancient technologies of the old ones."

While Rampa's story is admittedly difficult to take literally, it still works beautifully as a well-crafted bit of modern mythology, and Rampa's sincere, wide-eyed telling of the tale is so infectiously positive and uplifting that you end up feeling much better whether you believe it to be factual or not. In any case, he offers further testimony regarding the Inner Earth paradise and the earthly origin of flying saucers and must be taken seriously in those terms.

It is perhaps a universal human desire to find paradise on Earth, to collectively return to the Garden of Eden with the multiple sins of the multitudes forgiven. Perhaps this land of perfection and bliss we seek is indeed quite real, waiting for us beneath our feet and not somewhere out in the lonely stars.

SUGGESTED READING:

THE SMOKY GOD AND OTHER INNER EARTH MYSTERIES: UPDATED/EXPANDED EDITION

THE SECRET LOST DIARY OF ADMIRAL BYRD AND THE PHANTOM OF THE POLES

MY JOURNEY TO AGHARTA: THE LONG LOST BOOKS OF RAMPA

11

STRANGE THINGS ARE HAPPENING AROUND AND BENEATH MOUNT SHASTA
By Timothy Green Beckley

If you go back to California's newspaper archives over a century and a half, you will find news reports written by journalists with no ax to grind when it comes to one of the most beloved mysterious spots in the United States. Located in a community of just about 4,000, the pleasing locale attracts thousands of tourists every year who arrive to trail blaze up the multitude of paths that lead to Mount Shasta's picturesque summit.

They also come to meditate, sky watch for UFOs, say a telepathic hello to a friendly cryptid like Bigfoot, pay their respects to the ageless spiritual masters such as Count St. Germain or poke and probe the many crevices toward the top of the mount for an entrance to the Inner Earth, in particular the underground city of Telos which is located beneath Shasta, be it in a physical form or existing in another dimension or on the astral plane. Those "in the know," claim that Telos is part of a vast underground system with geological roots dating back to the lost Lemurian Empire, a "super civilization" located in the Pacific region in our planet's most remote past. .

Historically, credit is said to go to prospector J.C. Brown, a British national who came to Mount Shasta around 1900 and a few years later supposedly discovered a lost city beneath the mountain while in the employment of the Lord Cowdray Mining Company of England. Hired to prospect for gold, he hit "pay dirt" in a sense when he discovered a cave which sloped downward for eleven miles. He found an underground village there filled with valuable objects, such as golden shields and mummies, some being ten to twelve feet tall. Three decades went by and eventually a certain John C. Root organized an exploration team out of Stockton, California. Eighty people were on the team, but the day they were to be sent up the mountainside, Brown vanished and was never heard from again. And since no one possessed any maps as to where the cave entrance was located, the venture was scrapped.

Others have tried over the years to locate the "booty room," as it has been nicknamed, but have been unsuccessful in their quest. So all that wealth goes unclaimed, perhaps being guarded by underground dwellers who are often said to prevent surface dwellers from entering their cherished abode.

Located in close proximity to the Oregon border near the southern end of the Cascade Range in Siskiyou County and reaching an elevation of 14,180 feet, Mount Shasta is a potentially active volcano which last erupted in 1786. In order to access this mystical marvel of nature, visitors are apt to set up shop in any of the numerous motels or bed-and-breakfasts that dot the towns of Shasta and nearby Weed. They will undoubtedly stop in at one of the metaphysical bookstores like Soul Connections to get their bearings, perhaps purchase a crystal that has drawn itself to them or to network with others coming into the area for the first time, just like they are doing.

Some locals, as a suspected interloper may quickly find out, shy as far away as they can from discussing anything odd they may have seen or heard, feeling it attracts the wrong kind of tourist who come more for spiritual relief than to contribute to the economy. Instead of chowing down at a fancy restaurant they might, it is felt, want to head off to places like the local Buddhist monastery Shasta Abby, the "I Am" Pageant of the Angels, sponsored by the Saint Germain Foundation, or attended a private screening of "Dreams Awake." Written, produced and directed by Jerry Alden Deal, it is in essence the first feature film in a newly emerging cinematographic category known broadly as Transformational Media to be shot on location in and around Mount Shasta.

As it turns out, we recently came across the following decades-old account pertaining to the mysteries of Mount Shasta. The missive was written in 1946 in the form of a lengthy letter sent to Ray Palmer, then editor of "Amazing Stories." It was penned by Emma Martinelli, an active member of the San Francisco Interplanetary Club, and describes in copious detail the two weeks she spent on the slopes of Mount Shasta trying to sort through some of the most bizarre tales of metaphysical and orphic intrigue imaginable.

MORE MYSTERIES OF MOUNT SHASTA

"I have just returned from a two weeks stay in Weed, one of the towns which is about as near as you can get to Mount Shasta. The people in a small town are odd. I don't think you can crash them on a first entry. At least, I found this to be true, and I make friends very easily. I bided my time, and let them make the advances. Even after they took me in, I found most of them reluctant to talk about their 'mountain people.' Most of them apparently take little stock in the tales which are circulated. Some of them laugh, but I'm wondering if there might not be a few who know things they just don't want to talk about. Maybe they've had follow-up experiences after divulging previous occurrences. Your guess is as good as mine on this score.

The first movie to be shot entirely on Mount Shasta, "Dreams Awake" involves an ordinary family visiting the locale, only to be drawn into the spiritually of the mountain, including meditation practices, UFOs, the opening of a vortex, eventually meeting the ghostly figure of a young girl in the pines.

Prospector J.C. Brown (inset) claims to have discovered a huge treasure trove beneath Mount Shasta in a vast cavern. On the day they were supposed to head out to find this vast treasure, the head of the expedition disappeared and was never heard from again.

Stockton Record

FINAL HOME EDITION

80 STOCKTONIANS LEFT BEHIND IN SEARCH FOR 'LOST CONTINENT'

Followers Hold All-Night Vigil for Missing Leader on Trip to Find Weird Cave

Disappearance of "Chief" Leaves Group of Local People Enlisted in Mysterious Mission Pondering Next Step

Surprise Promised Unit Fails to Materialize While Many Hold Nocturnal Watch to Await J. C. Brown's Return

Here's Brown's Weird Tale of Lost "Village"

STOCKTONIANS LEFT BEHIND IN FANCY SEARCH

HERE'S BROWN'S WEIRD TALE OF LOST "VILLAGE"

Even the Native American tribes, as well as the earliest of settlers, realized there was something mystical about the mountain.

Invisible inhabitants, lost tribes, subterranean bell ringers and a medieval saint draw cultists to the mountain

BY ROBERT SPEER

The sects business is booming in **Mount Shasta City.**

Somewhat to the consternation of local old-timers, who tend toward orthodoxy in religious matters, this tidy community of 6,000 souls is mildly notorious for being the spiritual headquarters for more sects and

"I Am Come" Angel Pagent has been known to attract thousands who come to pay homage to the Ascended Master Count Saint Germain.

SECRET EXPLOITS OF ADMIRAL RICHARD E. BYRD

"I think I covered the town as well as anyone in my position could. It was a combination of practical judgment and vibration on my part. I left no stone unturned. I followed all leads and talked with others I felt led to talk to. Judge Bradley, a very old resident, knew nothing. Neither did the postmaster's mother, a Mrs. King. The most help I got was from a newspaper man, a Mr. Harder, who publishes the Weed 'Log,' and a clerk in the Log Cabin Hotel, an elderly gentleman who has lived in Weed for 27 years. His name is Bob Young.

"Harder was running the election at the time. He ran in on me on election morning, to relate an unusual experience which had just occurred. I have only his word for this, as I didn't see the creature involved. It seems that a sort of moron ambled into the place and said he just wanted to watch. Harder said he resembled a gorilla and was of a low order of intelligence. Harder was puzzled because he'd never seen this being before. In a town as small as this, a newcomer stands out like a sore thumb. Even the men from neighboring farms are somewhat familiar, if not actually known. This gorilla-type creature simply stood behind one of the girls who was counting votes and stared at her back. She became quite agitated and it was with difficulty that Harder finally got rid of this being. I hiked every day, alone in the woods, and never came across anyone like this.

"Even though I had no experiences to speak of the first few days, I was convinced that there was something around the Mountain, because I never felt alone. But it wasn't the nicest type of feeling. I felt as though I was being watched. The second day there I stumbled accidentally on a beautiful meadow. It was so perfect I wouldn't have been surprised to see fairies dance. I just lay face downwards to the earth and tried to relax, but I had to look around every so often. The stillness was unpleasant. It was too full of something unseen. You can walk all day long up there and not see a soul. And I constantly lost my way. I am a good hiker and I have a good sense of direction, but it seemed as though something were deliberately trying to confuse me. It's a very unpleasant feeling to realize that you are lost in a strange place. Each time this happened, I refused to become panicky and simply allowed myself to be led according to my inner light.

"I think there may be peculiar forces in the ground, because I saw a dog act very strangely. I was walking at sundown, and passed a cottage with a large red dog in front of it. I've been raised in the country with dogs and I think I know their habits fairly well. Many times they roll over and over in the earth, seeming to enjoy the fragrance, etc., but this dog had all the appearance of a dead animal. His legs were straight up in the air, paws rigid and even his mouth was fixed in a stiff position. I watched him for some time, then started for the cottage door to tell the occupants they had a dead dog. Just to be sure, I spoke to the dog first. This seemed to rouse him from his trance. He slithered through the half open gate and came over to where I stood. I patted his head and started on my way, but he put a paw on my arm. He didn't seem to want me to go, and he didn't look like an ordinary dog at all. He watched me all the way down the road, with the strangest expression in his eyes. I only mention this incident to bring out the fact that I think there may be certain currents in the earth.

THE SONG OF THE EARTH

"I wouldn't lay too much stock in this next incident, but I'll give it to you anyway. I'm a very practical person, and I always tear everything apart in analyzing it. I eliminate every material factor, and what is left I consider the truth. At least I'm able to know which experiences are fancied and which are not.

"I was awakened from sleep, by a peculiar scale of notes which seemed to come from under the bed. At first I thought it might just be the pounding of my heart. You know how you sometimes hear it in the pillow? But this was different. It sounded like a cross between the plucking of harp strings, and a very delicate anvil chorus. It sounded exactly like some sort of mechanism within the earth. I got it only once again some nights later, but much fainter. But there are three experiences which I know to be true; each happened when I least expected it.

"I had been there over a week and never walked at night. This particular evening I was very tired, but had the urge to go for a stroll. I took my flashlight and smokes, and sauntered down the highway towards the mountain. It was that peculiar half-light between day and night. There was only an egg shaped moon, and about three planets. As I neared a certain hill I happened to glance upward and saw a rocket-like affair heading toward a certain hill. It happened so quickly I wasn't able to digest it until afterward. I've seen Haley's comet and I've seen shooting stars, and it was neither. The nearest resemblance, though not exactly, was to a torch which might have been hurled from a plane. I thought, 'That's funny. Now who would want to set fire to the woods?' And then I realized that the mark would be missed anyhow, because this rocket affair disappeared over the hill. If it had gone down the swell, I'd have thought it landed on the other side, but it dissolved in mid-air.

"According to my scale of measurement, from where I was, this thing was visible for about three feet, appearing to come from the evening star, or whatever that first big planet was, going towards the moon which was nearer the hill, and then disappearing. I figure the disappearing doesn't mean it was no longer in flight. It just disappeared from my sight because there was no longer a visible propulsion. The head of this rocket was brighter than the tail, and the tail was composed of bright lines such as a jet propelled machined might leave in its wake. The hill over which it disappeared is just east of Mount Shasta. If this is what I think it was, I believe it kept going and landed right in the Mountain, much as a plane might fly into a hangar. My friend Harder went on a geologists' expedition up the mountain. He says there are caves in the glacier big enough to throw the community of Weed into! And I thought it very funny when I related this experience to

SECRET EXPLOITS OF ADMIRAL RICHARD E. BYRD

Known as "the man who lives forever," Saint Germain is the top ranking member of the Great White Brotherhood who materializes in the forest around Mount Shasta to spread his gospel of peace and harmony.

Shasta Abby, a Buddhist Monastery where all are welcome.

Out of range to all but the most adventuresome, this peak may lead downward
to the Inner Earth city of Telos.

Many tourists have observed UFOs over the mountain, some of which hide in lenticular clouds
just like in the movie "Close Encounters of the Third Kind."

Emporiums like the Soul Connections' Bookstore open their doors to those seeking wisdom and knowledge from far and wide.

Young. He looked at me very queerly and asked me on which side of the mountain this occurred. When I said the east side he smiled even more queerly. He said most everything occurred on that side.

"But here's the payoff. I came home immediately and wrote the experience to my sister. Wrote till nearly midnight, sealed the letter and retired. I arose in order to adjust the blind and rested my hand on the bedstead for support. I got such an electric shock that when I pulled my hand away I saw the sparks and heard them. I went over the floor for any exposed wires and found none. Tried to repeat the occurrence, but no soap.

THE VOICE FROM THE CAVERNS

"And here's the piece de resistance. I'll remember it much longer than the rest. I get goose pimples even now when I relate it.

"A couple of days later, just before returning to San Francisco, Young was telling me about a voice he used to hear across the way from the hotel. It seems he used to take a walk about six o'clock every evening. This spot is called the Pilgrim's Rest, and is in direct line with the room I occupied. There's a clean sweep of the mountain here. I could see it from my window. He said it was the anguished cry of a woman. I was determined to explore this very evening. Along about three thirty in the afternoon I became very drowsy and lay down for a nap. I dozed until five, and awakened. I lay with my eyes closed, in that relaxed state where you can't exactly collect your wits. Suddenly I was aware of voices, womenfolk's voices. They seemed to be faintly yelling. In my half stupor I thought there were young people playing outside. Then I remembered there were no young people here.

SECRET EXPLOITS OF ADMIRAL RICHARD E. BYRD

Now, one voice was predominant. It was a woman's voice. Rather thin and pathetic. It was more of an anguished call, than the type of scream accompanying a murder or such. It called, 'Help! Help! Help!' It was such an anguished cry for aid that I turned icy cold, and the minute I became taut it ceased. I was out of the bed like a shot out of a cannon. To be truthful I don't know whether the voice came from the ground under the bed, or across the way from the mountain. I'm inclined to think it came from the mountain.

"But here's the difference between these last two experiences: the rocket incident was objective, the voice subjective. Anyone with me would have seen the flare. I'm not sure that anyone with me would have heard the voice. Young says the same; no one ever seemed to hear what he heard. Last of all, I'm curious to know if I was supposed to see this flare, or was it an accident?

"There you are, Mr. Palmer. As much as I can give you. I tried my darnedest to climb that mountain, but no marked trails, and they simply wouldn't let me go alone. I'd make trouble for them if I got lost, freeze to death in the night, etc. To tell you the truth I'm glad I couldn't go. I'm not ashamed to be afraid of such things. I

Among the many strange and wonderous creatures claimed to have been seen near Mt. Shasta is the enigmatic and ever-elusive "Big Foot."

figure I didn't do too badly for a newcomer. The geologists' expedition found nothing at all. They had University of California men with them and all the necessary equipment, tapped all over the mountain and explored thoroughly. I think this proves that only those who are ready for such experiences have them. It's not so much a case of being equipped materially, but being equipped psychically. Of course I'm in favor of an armed expedition to clean out the Dero, but I don't think any but righteously advanced people can contact the good forces. In signing off, I'm here to tell you that you have a jewel in Shaver. What he doesn't know — isn't worth knowing. Let those who want to laugh, laugh. I'll take vanilla."

Emma was making a guarded reference to the very disturbing writings of the late Richard Sharpe Shaver, who for years before his passing in 1976 said that he and millions of others, who were thought to be mentally deranged but were not, were hearing voices from deep underground, utterances made by a mutated race who abducted humans from the surface only to cannibalize their flesh or turn them into submissive slaves. Shaver described in blatant terms, in articles published in the pulp magazines of the 1940s and early 50s, this hellish realm of fire and brimstone and the entrance ways of a vast cavern system controlled by the Dero. One entrance would be via an elevator in a Manhattan office skyscraper, which went down well below basement level, beyond the prying eyes of employees who did not know the code to get the elevator to go sideways into an almost bottomless shaft leading to the Inner Earth.

Luckily, we are told that in and around Mount Shasta the Dero had been kept in check by a benevolent race Shaver identified as the Tero, who were not bent on destroying the outer earth dwellers (that would be us), but wished to live in peace and harmony with us. I guess the Tero acted as a "watchdog" group for the residents of Telos, who are known to be pacifists.

Other sections of this book will deal with the Shaver Mystery in more detail as we continue with the words of Emma, our guide for the moment in and around Mount Shasta.

SIX YEARS LATER

In 1952 Emma stopped in Weed on her return from British Columbia, in company with her sister and brother-in-law. She continues: "We had parked the car in a direct line with the hotel room I had occupied six years previously. I was not hungry, so while the others went into the hotel for luncheon I remained in the car writing a letter. Suddenly smoke rose from the car floor. I thought this strange as I was not smoking a cigarette at the time. On looking down I discovered that a hole had been burned right through the car carpet! Naturally I immediately rubbed out the scorch and burn with my foot. The only visible physical cause would be the rather warm high noon sun shining through a bottle of mineral water on the floor, but in view of such a possibility I had covered this jug with my sweater. Even with the summer sun, it would seem illogical that within a few minutes of parking, and with the shielded bottle, that a fire of this nature would be started. Some may say the mineral water contained an element which augmented the sun's rays. My guess would be, in view of previous findings, that if anything augmented the solar rays through a heavily covered bottle it was a booster current or magnetic ray from underground, as this was the exact spot where the episodes occurred six years previously.

"A word might not be amiss here, in regard to any cavern world. I think that the Director of BSRA (an acronym for the Borderland Sciences Research Association) has the most balanced viewpoint as evidenced by his material about the Inner Earth. He does not say that the Inner Earth cannot be inhabited by physical or dimensionally interchangeable beings. He does not say they are all good or all bad. He merely hints, in substance, that unless we can do a thorough job in cleaning out the undesirable, it is better not to stir up a hornet's nest.

"I visited Shasta territory again in 1953, staying in the town of Mount Shasta, nine miles south of Weed on Highway 99 and more to the east. I have come a long way since 1945 and this I have found, we may have the good OR the bad. Our own thinking process is the port of entry I brought back preponderance of good from the beautiful Mt. Shasta, not evil. Good which has stayed with me through the years."

In fact, the head of the BSRA and editor of his then widely-read monthly publication at the time, Meade Layne noted: "Shasta is a mountain of mystery, as Emma's 1946 visit proved to her. Your Editor has little reason to doubt that a Lodge of the White Brotherhood is active there. My study of the Kabala has taught me the principle of balance. This means that there must be also a Lodge of Black Magicians in the Shasta area. I have been told that this Lodge occupies 6,000 foot Black Butte, next to Mount Shasta – on which cinder pile nothing seems to want to grow. If your curiosity about Shasta has been aroused by the reading of this material, by all means visit the place if you can.

"The mountain is an impressive pile of white, standing by itself against the California sky. Judy and I spent one night in the town of Shasta on the western slopes of the mountain, during our February 1961 lecture trip up to Vancouver and back. We didn't experience anything unusual and would have liked to stay longer to get the feel of the place. There are plenty of good motels in Shasta and Weed. There is also a comparatively new ski lodge on the mountain at about the 7,000 ft. level, with an excellent paved road going up to it from Shasta. The ski lift goes on up to about 9,000 feet, and operates in the summer as well. Accommodations at the lodge are limited and not cheap; reservations have to be made in advance during the winter skiing season. We would have liked to spend our night up there but the lodge is closed on Monday and Tuesday and booked solid the rest of the week. In my estimation, Mount Shasta has been a center for occult activity here on the Pacific Coast for thousands of years. For this reason, powerful elemental forces, neither good nor bad in themselves, continually play in and around the mountain. Individual reaction to these forces will depend on the preponderance of good or evil in one's own personality!"

SUGGESTED READING AND WEB SITES

MOUNT SHASTA AND A DWELLER ON TWO PLANETS

MYSTERIES OF MT SHASTA: HOME OF THE UNDERGROUND DWELLERS

SUBTERRANEAN WORLDS INSIDE EARTH

INNER EARTH PEOPLE, OUTER SPACE PEOPLE

RICHARD SHAVER: REALITY OF THE INNER EARTH

HIDDEN WORLD SERIES (Edited by Ray Palmer)

Shasta Abbey Buddhist Monastery – www. ShastaAbbet,Org

Saint Germain Foundation – www.saintgermainfoundation.org/

Soul Connections "Emporium" – ectionsStore.com/"

www.SoulConnectionsStore.com

BSRA – www.BorderlandSciences.org" www.BorderlandSciences.org

Spiritual Tourism and Frontier Esotericism at Mount Shasta, Madeline Duntley – Bowling Green University (Google To Find PDF).

12

EXPLORE MOUNT SHASTA AND ENTER AN UNKNOWN KINGDOM – CALIFORNIA'S GATEWAY TO ANOTHER REALM
By Timothy Green Beckley

I have known Dianne Robbins for so long I can't remember how long I've known her . . .

Now I know that's a rather silly, somewhat embarrassing statement, but one tends to get caught up in matters beyond the mundane when it comes to "shop talk" on the Inner Earth.

When I first started corresponding with Dianne she was living in upstate New York, around Rochester I think it was, and her profession was that of a school teacher. Someone must have turned her on to the rock band the Moody Blues, and shortly thereafter her "straight-laced" image of being an instructor to high schoolers was blown. But let her tell us this little story:

"*As a child I used to stand outside and look up at the night sky, and wonder where, in the starry heavens above, was my home. In 1990, when I was listening to music of the Moody Blues and heard their song, 'I Know You're Out There Somewhere,' it suddenly flooded me with memories and I instantly knew there was a whole other dimension out there just waiting to communicate with me. I began a process of meditation that reawakened me to the remembrance that I am a telepathic receiver and transmitter for the Inner-Earth terrestrials, Cetaceans, Crystal Kingdom, Tree People and Nature Kingdoms. I also awakened to my divine mission and role for this lifetime*"

No doubt the harsh winters of upstate New York had something to do with her decision to make a radical physical move to California, where she settled as near to Mount Shasta as a person could possibly do without having been born and raised there in a tepee like our late friend, the Native American, Bleu Ocean. My longtime friend just so happens also to have led a life as a real rock and roller, having worked for Pink Floyd and others as an all-around session drummer. (In the previous work "Mysteries of Mount Shasta" we detailed Bleu's many experiences related to this magical mountain, of great spiritual significance to so many, that is located near the Oregon border).

SECRET EXPLOITS OF ADMIRAL RICHARD E. BYRD

This move, in many ways, acted as an electrifying moment in her life's work, as she found that she had the ability to speak telepathically with the highly advanced "good souls," whom she says reside inside Mount Shasta, a place known to those in the New Age community as the home of the Ascended Masters. This race of underground beings, much like us in physical appearance, desire to spread their knowledge and wisdom to those living on the outside of the planet, so that we can learn to live in harmony with Gaia before we end up annihilating ourselves.

"Much of my inspiration comes from communing with Nature through long walks in the woods, sitting under my favorite tree in my backyard, walking along the ocean when I'm in Florida, and being on the mountain among the trees on Mt. Shasta, California, my home"

Some of the central figures she communicates with include Adama in the Subterranean City of Telos, Mikos in the Hollow Earth, several Ascended Masters, the Ashtar Command of the Confederation of Planets, and various nature spirits.

"I no longer felt alone, but suddenly connected to Beings everywhere through the telepathic phone lines that exist throughout the cosmos. My communication with Mikos has reconnected me to who I am, and why I am here, and I discovered that I am connected to all life - everywhere - not just on Earth but all life forms throughout our Milky Way."

A HOW-WHO OF THE INNER EARTH

Dianne Robbins has self-determined the wheres and whatfors of the place and the dwellers of the inner earth whom she is so at ease and in league with:

"Not just our Earth, but all planets are hollow! Planets are formed by hot gases thrown from a sun into an orbit, and the shell of planets is created by gravity and centrifugal forces, and the POLES REMAIN OPEN and lead to a hollow interior.

"This process forms a hollow sphere with an Inner Sun, smoky in color, which gives off soft and pleasant full spectrum sunlight, making the inside surface highly conducive to growth of vegetation and Human life, with only a long-long day and no nights.

"The HOLLOW EARTH BEINGS are very spiritually evolved and technologically advanced, and live inside the interior core of our Hollow Earth.

"These advanced civilizations live in peace and brotherhood in the Center of our Earth, which contains an Inner Central Sun with oceans and mountains still in their pristine state.

"The Hollow Earth cavity is still in its pristine state, because they don't walk or build upon their land. There are no buildings, shopping malls or highways. They travel in electromagnetic vehicles that levitate a few inches above ground.

"They walk along streams, rivers, and oceans and climb mountains - but that's

the extent of their foot contact with the ground. They leave the rest of their land to nature, because it's nature's land too.

"The force of gravity in the Inner Earth is half that of the outer surface, which may be one explanation for the greater height of the people, plants and the trees; some of their Redwoods reach over a thousand feet in height.

"The source of Earth's magnetic field has been a mystery. The Inner Sun at the center of Earth is the mysterious power source behind the Earth's magnetic field.

"There are entry caverns all over the Earth, where interactions can take place. Only some are currently open. Nikola Tesla, the genius inventor of electrical technology, is now living inside the Hollow Earth.

"He began to receive information in the latter part of the 1800's and discovered that: "electric power is everywhere present in unlimited quantities and can drive the world's machinery without the need of coal, oil, gas or any other of the common fuels."

"In the 1930's the tunnel entrances and passageways were closed off by the Hollow Earth civilizations, because 'corporations' at that time were misusing Tesla's technology to gain entrance into the Inner Earth.

"The Hollow Earth's two main Portals are at the Holes at the Poles, which were closed off in the year 2000 because our governments were setting detonations at the Poles to blow open entrances into their world."

ADAMA OF TELOS TALKS OF HIS EXPERIENCE OF VISITING
THE OCEANS AND MOUNTAINS WITHIN THE INNER EARTH CAVITY

But why don't we go directly to the source for our information on the city beneath Mount Shasta and the world of the Inner Earth people? For this we need Dianne to engage in a channeling session with the very "anatomically correct" Adama, who looks, according to the portraits that have been rendered of him, like he just stepped off the set of a daytime soap opera drama. The channeled information:

The Earth's interior is the mirror image of the surface foundation. Everything is in reverse order inside of the Earth. The mountain ranges are in direct proportion to the dimensions of the Earth's cavity and tower above the landscape.

The oceans are larger than life and flow calmly and swiftly around the inside of the globe. The air is crisp and clean, and the sand is white. The Central Sun is dimmer than the sun on the outside and reflects the Light from the Heavens.

The cities are all nestled in lush woodlands, overflowing with flowers and huge trees. There is green growth surrounding all manmade structures. Everything is in perpetual blossom and bloom. It is a land of wonder and beauty.

All is in perfect proportion to the size of the circumference of the interior. Everything is larger than life – even the great Beings who inhabit the interior are

Adama

larger than the mortals on the outside. All is beauty, and all is in a heavenly state of bliss.

Just picture the interior foundtion reflecting the exterior foundation; with mountain ranges higher, and the ocean currents swifter, and the green land growth lush beyond compare. You do not need to picture a change in the contour of the land.

It is still in its pristine beauty, and replicates how life on the surface once was. The exact location of the mountain ranges and oceans is not necessary to know at this time. What is necessary to know is that this Inner World exists, and co-exists with the surface, under peaceful and contrary conditions....

The Hollow Earth is a Paradise, with tall, graceful mountains jutting into the "sky," and large, clear, clean lakes and oceans that abound with life. The diet in the Hollow Earth is strictly vegetarian, and people are healthy, robust, and strong.

They, too, have isolated themselves from the surface population, although they come and leave the Earth freely using the spacecraft that are kept there in the Spaceport inside of the Earth. So although they are inside the Earth, they have freedom and health and abundance and peace – all the necessary components of life that you on the surface have been crying out for.

There is free travel between the subterranean cities and the Hollow Earth through the tunnels, using our electromagnetic trains that can take us from one part of the Earth to another in a fraction of the time it takes you on the surface. Our transportation is quick and efficient and burns no fuels. Therefore, there's no pollution underground.

WE LIVE INSIDE CAVERN HOMES FROM WHICH
WE CAN LOOK OUT ONTO OUR GREEN WORLD OUTSIDE

Another popular channeler from the depths, Mikos, adds these thoughts:

Now that you are somewhat familiar with the Hollow Earth, we can "dig" further into your credibility and introduce another factor of our living arrangements underground.

Underground, we do not live out in the open spaces the way you do on the surface. Our Hollow Earth cavity is pristine, because we don't tread upon her inner surface nor build upon her.

We don't have shopping malls and expanses of highways nor towering buildings. We live inside caverns, with openings facing outward towards the open, wide spaces of the Hollow cavity inside the Earth.

Sure, we travel inside the cavity on our electromagnetic vehicles that levitate a few inches above the ground, never touching the ground.

We walk softly on the earthen paths and run along the streams, rivers and oceans, and climb the towering mountains. But that is the extent of our foot contact

SECRET EXPLOITS OF ADMIRAL RICHARD E. BYRD

Dianne Roberts,
Paranormal Investigator
at Mt. Shasta.

with the terrain. The rest we leave to Nature's Devas and Elementals, as it is their land, too.

All our living activity takes place within our inner caverns, which are vast and wide and high and composed of crystalline rocks and gemstones and crystal arches radiating full-spectrum colored rainbows of sparkling light into our cavern atmosphere. Our walls are lined with natural rainbow-hued waterfalls, humidifying the air with the vibrancy and song of its water cascading down.

Yes, our water "sings" – and its chorus brings our body cells into harmony, so that our bodies are always vibrating to our water and crystalline surroundings that keep us energized and vibrant all day long. We need little sleep, because our cells are always tuned and in harmony to the natural rhythm of Mother Earth herself.

When you are tuned like a tuning fork, then you carry the full life force of our Mother, and your battery never runs down. Hence, there is little need for the long hours of sleep such as you experience.

You are drained and run-down after a day in your "sweatshops," but we are always as vibrant at the end of our days as we are when we begin them. We live "in" and "with" the Earth, whereas you live "outside" and "separate" from her. Hence, you are "cut off," while we are a "part" of her. This is the big difference.

Your Spiritual Hierarchy has been preparing housing for you inside these vast, uninhabited caverns in Earth's interior, and when the external "Earth

Changes" come, many of you will be moved en masse into them to continue your present incarnation inside Earth, not "on" her.

You will encounter a "whole" new way of living that is wholesome and rich and perfect in every way. It will expand your consciousness and expand your horizon, and your horizon will be an inner horizon vaster than when you walk outdoors on the surface. A whole new horizon is waiting for you to experience.

Events will start happening fast now, as time is speeding up even faster as world karma is playing itself out. Just ride with the tide and know you are safe wherever you are.

You are all being directed and guided from within, and you are all being provided for. What you witness through your media is only a "play," a drama that they want you to believe is real, just because the actors are real.

But the actors are just "playing out their part" in the world's drama, and this is the biggest "hit" yet of the new Millennium playing on your TV and movie theater screens everywhere. Just turn the knob off, go within yourself, and feel and focus on World Peace. Peace is the real movie, and the only "reel" to watch.

Soon, you will see us, and soon you, too, will be living perfectly suited to

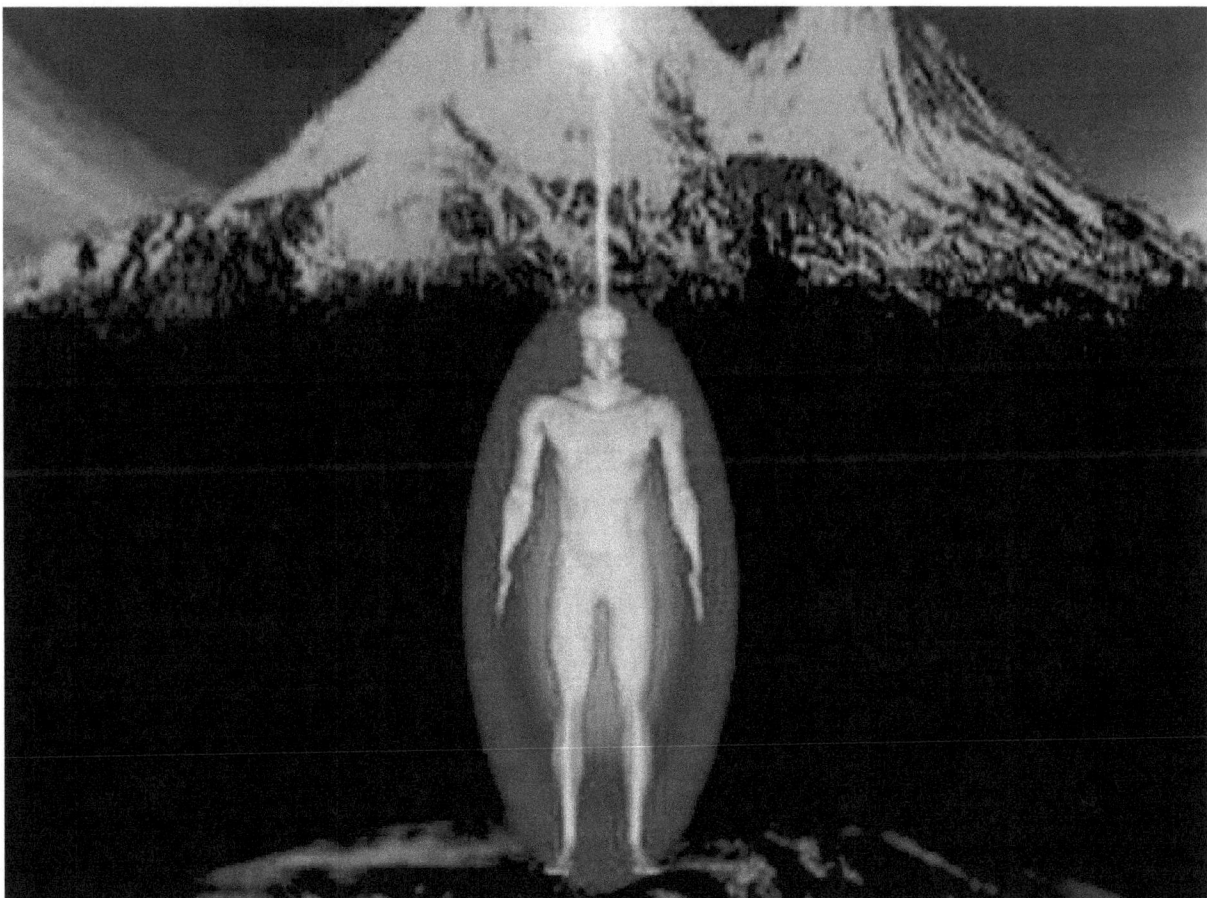

your new way of life.

DO TELOS AND OTHER CITIES
IN THE INNER EARTH EXIST PHYSICALLY?

We will answer your question. Yes and no. Yes, Telos does exist in your Third Dimension, and it also exists in the Fifth Dimension. It actually does physically exist inside of Mt. Shasta in the Third Dimension. There are no volcano activities inside of Mt. Shasta.

The lava tunnels in Mt. Shasta were re-routed by us over 12,000 years ago when the Lemurians went underground and traveled through the tunnels to reside in Mt. Shasta as a result of the Atlantean and Lemurian Wars which devastated the surface.

So we do exist in our Third Dimensional body forms which we can now move in and out of at will. We have evolved to the point where we can raise and lower our energy fields and move in and out of embodiment. So if you were in Telos in your Third Dimensional form, you would see us.

However, when we come up to the outside of the Mountain, we modify our energy field and move up to the Fifth Dimension and are "shielded" from your physical eyes, unless you can see into the Fifth Dimension. If you can perceive the Fifth Dimension energy, then you would see us. And yes, we look exactly like you.

There are no differences in our physical bodies, except for the fact that we now have more DNA strands as a result of our long lives of being able to evolve in peace and harmony and brotherhood.

For it takes a peaceful environment to evolve, and this is what we created for ourselves when we left the surface and came into Mt. Shasta.

When we want to be seen by those on the outside of the Mountain, we can easily make ourselves visible to you.

But for the most part, we prefer to stay invisible for our own protection. The time will come when we will be appearing to your surface folk, and that time is very near. We hope this has answered your question. I am Mikos.

WHAT IS THE DIFFERENCE BETWEEN
THE INNER EARTH AND THE HOLLOW EARTH?

The Inner Earth consists of Telos and over 120 other Agartha Subterranean Cities of Light just a few miles beneath Earth's surface, including the city of Catharia, which is directly inside the center core of the Earth (beneath the Aegean Sea) and is where the Library of Porthologos is located and where Mikos is from.

The Inner Earth consists of all the area that is below the Earth's surface throughout the globe, including caverns and a vast tunnel system. It includes all 800 miles from the top of the Earth's surface to the inner hollow opening in the center.

Paranormal Investigator Dianne Roberts explores the mystery and adventure of Mt. Shasta in California

The Hollow Earth is just the area that exists in the very center core of the Earth, which is Hollow, and starts at 800 miles down. Once you are inside the hollow cavity of Earth, the diameter of open space is 6,400 miles. The diameter of the whole Earth is 8,000 miles.

WHY ARE WE SKIPPING THE FOURTH DIMENSION
WHEN WE MOVE INTO THE FIFTH DIMENSION?

We will all attempt to answer this question, because it is a complex one. We are the Inner Earth Council, Mikos presiding.

We say to you not to be so caught up in dimensions, but rather to concentrate on bringing up your energy and raising it up into higher levels of consciousness, because this is where the higher dimensions exist. They exist in higher states of awareness. So you can access higher dimensions by accessing higher states of consciousness.

You will move directly into the Fifth Dimension, because the Fourth Dimension will no longer exist.

It is in the process of being dismantled and removed by the Spiritual Hierarchy as part of the accelerated Ascension Plan that will catapult you directly into the Fifth Dimension.

The Fourth Dimension was used in the past by departing souls who didn't go directly to the Light but lingered for great lengths of time.

This departure passageway has now changed, or has been "re-routed," as you might say, so that departing souls no longer become trapped in obsolete dimensions waiting for hundreds or thousands of years to move on to the Light. That is now all over with. Therefore, you will all move directly up to the Fifth, with no dimensions in between.

The next step is wherever you want to put your foot. After you reach Fifth Dimensional consciousness and are securely in the Fifth Dimension, you will then choose your future destination at that time.

Some of you may choose to return to a Third Dimensional world to help other souls regain their full consciousness, and some of you may choose to go back to your Home Planets.

Your Home Planets exist in many different dimensions throughout the Universe, depending on how evolved your Soul is.

Your Soul's frequency matches your planet's frequency. So, yes, some of you may choose to go home to your Sixth Dimensional Planet and some may choose to go home to your Seventh Dimensional Planet and some of you may choose to go home to your Eighth Dimensional Planet and so on.

Do you understand this? Many Souls may want to stay in the Fifth Dimension and experience its peacefulness and abundance and riches and continue their soul advancement there for a while before moving on.

There will be a myriad of choices once you reach the Fifth Dimension, so there is no need to concern yourself about this now or try to make decisions about where you want to go. There is no hurry.

The only hurry is to reach the Fifth Dimensional Plane of existence, where you will be once again pain free, disease free, lack free, and totally free in all ways

. You will be supplied with all you could ever wish for, and then more. So stay tuned into your consciousness, be alert to all that is around you, make positive and loving choices, and send love to everyone. This is the fastest way to increase your awareness and evolve your consciousness.

Always remember that we in the Inner Earth are all standing beside you,

SECRET EXPLOITS OF ADMIRAL RICHARD E. BYRD

gently guiding you on your path to the Stars.

More References: www.DianneRobbins.com, www.TheNewEarth.org

["Messages from the Hollow Earth" – Channeled, published and distributed by: Dianne Robbins - Box 825, Weed, CA 96094 USA.

TelosMtShasta@gmail.com]

SUGGESTED READING —

BOOKS BY DIANNE ROBBINS

TELO

MESSAGES FROM THE HOLLOW EARTH

THE CALL GOES OUT

TREE TALK

MESSAGES FROM CRYSTAL KINGDOM

Odd lenticular clouds in a variety of sizes, shapes and colors
are forever forming over Mt. Shasta. Some theorists claim these are really
psychically induced images of "flying saucers."

13

THE PRIVATE HELL OF RICHARD SHAVER AND THE COMING OF THE SAUCERS
By Sean Casteel

There is an ancient occult adage that goes "As Above, So Below" and while not directly related to the content of this book, it could justifiably be used to describe our interest in unexplainable phenomena on and above the planet's surface, as well as what might well be taking place just a few feet to a mile or more "down under."

Biblically, for those who put their faith in the Holy Bible, The Book of Ecclesiastes in the Old Testament decries repeatedly "the evil that is done under the sun," but what if there is also great evil done beneath the surface of the Earth? I have written previously about how flying saucers may originate from an Inner Earth paradise, but the late author and "victim" Richard Shaver would doubtless offer a vigorous protest to that idea.

For Shaver, as with most percipients of the paranormal, the strange experiences began in his childhood. In a book from Timothy Green Beckley's Global Communications/Inner Light Publications called "Richard Shaver: Reality of the Inner Earth," edited by Tim R. Swartz, Shaver describes hearing horrifying disembodied voices as a young boy.

"From as far back as I can remember," Shaver writes, "there were the voices. They weren't there all the time, but they were there enough that they played an important role in my early childhood development. At first I thought that everyone heard the voices. I thought there was nothing strange about being awakened at night with the hideous screams of someone being torn limb from limb ringing in your ears. I thought it was normal to hear the maniacal laughing of an invisible someone who thought it was a fine joke to see an innocent soul run down by a speeding train. I thought everyone knew that the voices were with us all of the time, watching, waiting, scheming for our bloody deaths. But I was wrong. It seemed that I was the only one who heard the voices. I learned quickly not to talk about them, lest I be thought a maniac."

SECRET EXPLOITS OF ADMIRAL RICHARD E. BYRD

Shaver's voices gradually faded from his life and became only a distant childhood memory. They returned, however, when he was an adult working at an auto plant in Detroit. He began to hear them through the noise of the machinery, conversing among themselves about gleefully tearing the skin off a woman as she screamed for mercy or causing cars and planes to crash.

He concluded he must be quite insane, quit his job, began to live a hobo life and took to alcohol to try to block the voices out. He found himself confined to a prison or mental hospital – he seems unclear on which – and came to believe the voices came from people living in caves beneath the institution where he was incarcerated, tormenting him and the other prisoners with strange technologies he compared to some kind of x-rays.

THE MENTALLY INSANE

Shaver writes: "My problems, I realized, did not stem from some kind of mental impairment. I wasn't crazy in the traditional sense, even though at times I felt like I was being driven mad by the hateful rays that were being beamed at me by the people below. No, I was sane in an insane world.

"I have often wondered," he continues, "how many people who have been institutionalized because they were diagnosed as crazy were in fact victims, such as myself, of the damnable rays. Did they themselves think that they were insane because of the voices they heard in their heads and voluntarily committed themselves? Even today I still wonder if most forms of mental illness are not actually insidious attacks from the world below."

Over time, perhaps as a method of coping with the voices, Shaver began to develop a myth or a narrative to explain them. He writes about the coming of the "Titans," a humanoid race that migrated from their home planet and settled on Earth long before mankind was created. The Titans created the first civilization on the Earth, a social and scientific utopia that has never been equaled since.

But there came a time when the sun began to flare in dangerous ways and Earth was flooded with world-destroying radiation. The Titans had no choice but to flee, but some of them stubbornly refused to abandon their homes and instead moved underground or beneath the seas. They took their great machines and scientific knowledge with them, in hopes of someday finding a solution to the solar radiation and returning to live on the Earth's surface.

But even deep within the Earth, the solar radiation continued to affect them. They tried moving deeper into the planet, but to no avail.

"Those who did not die immediately," Shaver writes, "suffered genetic damage that was passed down from generation to generation. Eventually, this once mighty race was reduced to mutated horrors, retarded in intelligence and social structure. Worse still, these monstrosities still had access to the self-repairing machines of their ancestors. But instead of using them for their intended purposes,

Richard Shaver sits in his study chomping on his pipe.

Rare photo of Richard Shaver and publisher Ray Palmer side by side, along with other leading lights of the field.

The original "Shaver Mystery Magazine" has mutated just like the Dero before them in Rich Toronto's "Shavertron" online publication.

Secret, mysterious tunnels, rivers and fabulous cities beneath our feet!

Worlds of perpetual splendor are hidden within the Hollow Earth!

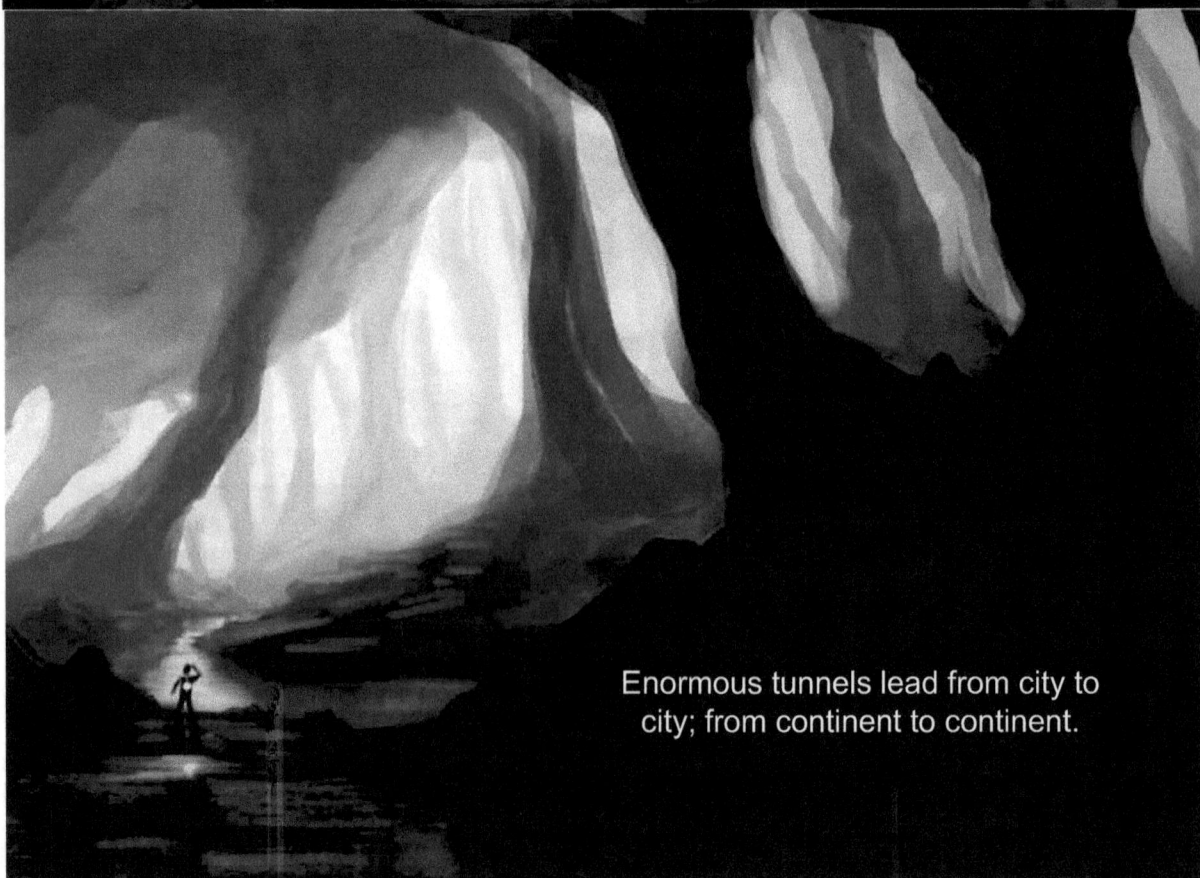

Enormous tunnels lead from city to city; from continent to continent.

Everything is light. There is a kind of twilight, but no darkness.

Mutant art: Head and shoulders of a "Dero."

A dastardly bunch, the Dero are pictured abducting humans forsadistic purposes. Art by Carol Ann Rodriguez.

they used them to satisfy their sick, twisted desires. These are the demons of ancient myth and folklore."

Shaver eventually began to write about this complex and bizarre scenario and sent a letter to a pulp sci-fi magazine called "Amazing Stories" in late 1943. At the time, the much-celebrated Ray Palmer was the editor, and he writes about discovering Shaver in another Global Communications release called "The Hidden World, Volume One," part of a series of books consisting of Shaver's collected writings.

"One day a letter came in," Palmer recalls, "giving the details of an 'ancient alphabet' that 'should not be lost to the world.' It was opened by my managing editor, Howard Browne, who read it with typical orthodox attitude and tossed it in the wastebasket with the comment, 'The world is full of crackpots.' Even through the intervening wall I heard his remark, and the word 'crackpot' drew me like a magnet."

Palmer began to experiment with the ancient alphabet, said to be the basis of all known human language, and realized the language system Shaver had written about actually worked. Palmer published the letter in "Amazing Stories," which quickly made pulp magazine publishing history. Hundreds of letters poured in asking where Shaver had gotten his alphabet. Shaver answered by submitting a 10,000 word manuscript, poorly typed and entitled "A Warning To Future Man."

Palmer read the manuscript through and then asked himself what it was he had exactly? It was not a simple matter of an author trying to make a sale. Shaver wanted no money for his manuscript, which was really more accurately a letter written as a warning. Shaver was anxious that it be published, not for notoriety but out of a sincere desire that the world be warned of the terrible danger it faced and informed of a wonderful heritage it had lost and which should be recovered if at all possible.

TOO AMAZING FOR 'AMAZING STORIES'?

Palmer said the manuscript was problematic for "Amazing Stories." It was not a story about the future, based on factual science, the usual fare for the magazine. Shaver's manuscript instead purported to be about the science of the past. But Palmer saw that here was a "jumping off place" for some really terrific stories, and with his mind focused on potential profits for the magazine if the stories were properly packaged and promoted on the cover, he began to rewrite Shaver's manuscript into a longer story entitled "I Remember Lemuria."

Palmer says he did not alter the "factual" basis of Shaver's manuscript but changed the story so that it did not revolve around literal caves in the Earth with actual people living there but instead was the product of "racial memory," a story encoded into Shaver's DNA from eons past. The point in doing this was to make it more believable to the magazine's readers, but the results went surprisingly beyond initial expectations.

Not only did readers find Shaver's story believable, they did so in unprecedented numbers. The issue of "Amazing Stories" that included "I Remember Lemuria" sold out its first press run of 135,000 copies, but this during World War II and even pulp paper was rationed by law. But through some shady dealing and with the help of Shaver's underground "contacts," sufficient paper was obtained to print another 50,000 copies, which sold out overnight. The enormous popularity of what came to be called the "Shaver Mysteries" had begun.

But that popularity did not come without some nay-saying. The readers of "Amazing Stories" were hardcore sci-fi buffs who weren't interested in some fantasy story that claimed to be true. They of course wrote to the magazine in protest. Meanwhile, one of the owners of the publishing company that included "Amazing Stories" in its empire of pulp magazines, Bernard Davis, called to say the extra 50,000 copies had been printed without the approval of higher ups and predicted they would not sell nor would the usual customers buy the first printing either. Of Shaver's story, Davis said, "I have never read such balderdash in my life."

Nevertheless, a total of around 50,000 people wrote letters praising "I Remember Lemuria," with many of them claiming to hear the same voices Shaver was hearing. Palmer writes of visiting Shaver at his home in Pennsylvania and reporting that he also heard voices as he lay in bed long after Shaver had retired for the night.

The complete text of "I Remember Lemuria" is reprinted in "The Hidden World, Volume One," and if you've never read it, it should go to the top of your "must-read" list. It's the one that started the whole ball rolling and is a classic work of occult lore. Historically, there are few things as significant to the entire field of Inner Earth belief.

Returning to Shaver's underground cosmology, the mutated, horrific creatures he described were given the name "Dero," which is a combination of the words "detrimental" and "robot." Another variation is "degenerate robot." Shaver said we were all a "Dero" to some degree, descended from the same genetic stock, but that the actual underground dwellers took their evil to such extremes that there was virtually no comparison.

The Dero not only caused wicked mayhem on the surface, such as wars and genocide and mass perversions and all forms of sadistic cruelty, it was also their primary pleasure, their reason for existence, their true joy in living. With their advanced technology, some of it capable of total mind control and even a kind of demonic possession, the Dero were far more powerful than mankind's ability to resist and overcame our puny efforts at righteousness with a gleeful, supernatural ease.

THE PROBLEM OF EVIL

This is, of course, a 20th century restatement of the age-old "Problem of Evil." Why, if God is our benevolent, loving Father, does evil exist with such a rigorous, insurmountable force? If we are made in God's image, why are we, collectively, so screwed up? Shaver's answer, that the Dero are to blame, seems as logical as any other attempt to explain the sorry state of the world. His Dero are an acceptable variation on the theme of a deceiving Satan who caused mankind's fall from grace in Eden and has made war on us ever since. Shaver's monsters are also located in the hollows of the Earth itself, which is where hell is said to be located by believers in religion and mythology throughout the world and down through history.

Shaver successfully combined both ancient and familiar elements with a new modern urgency that was both original and very marketable, as the continued success reaped by Palmer and his publishing house bore witness to. Shaver began to write more stories about the Dero in 1944 and had a long and profitable run with them. But the sci-fi buffs remained irate about the intrusion of nonfiction into their precious "Amazing Stories," and in 1948, in spite of the fact that he had

**Bill Birnes and John Rhodes
Dulce, New Mexico. Feb. 2, 2009**

Richard Shaver would be proud of these inner earthers and their work to put the subject before the public.

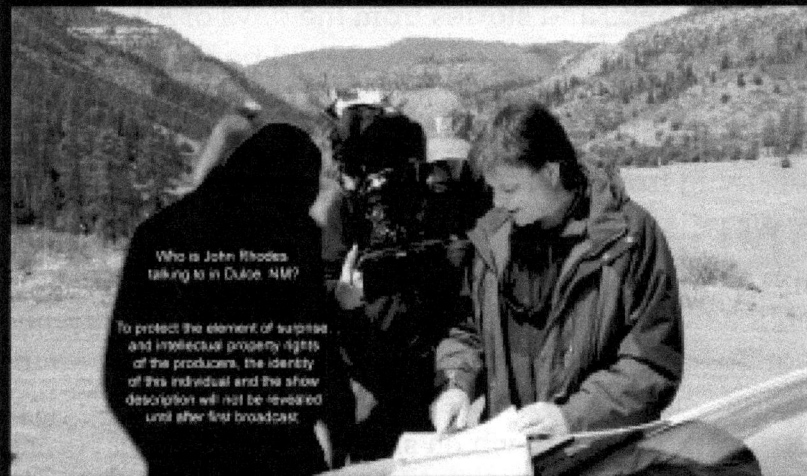

Who is John Rhodes talking to in Dulce, NM?

To protect the element of surprise, and intellectual property rights of the producers, the identity of this individual and the show description will not be revealed until after first broadcast.

John Rhodes

Did You Know? Once in Dulce, NM, an entire elementary school PE class and teacher witnessed a 3 foot tall creature (appearing like a wrinkled old man with almond eyes, a quill-like beard and no shoes) burst though the doors into the gym, gasping, shrieking, and began running from corner to corner in fear. The room turned to panic, and the teacher quickly got the children out of the gym, and shut the doors. After the school staff was gathered, they decided to open the doors and give whatever ran inside an opportunity to escape. The doors were left open unattended, so no one saw it leave (if it actually did!) Now there is a new elementary school and gym, but the old one where this happened is not used much as the locals believe it is taboo, or bad luck, to go into there. John Rhodes confirmed this event as authentic with local Jicarilla Apache residents on 04/04/14.

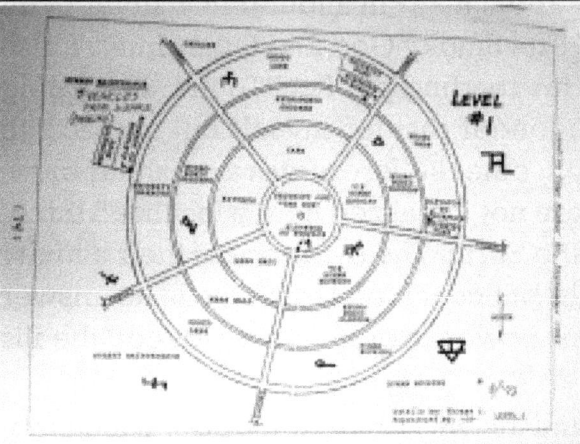

PAUL BENNEWITZ DULCE MAP

built up the circulation to 200,000 a month, a figure unheard of for most pulp magazines of that era, Palmer decided to strike off on his own, having grown tired of the friction the situation was causing. That same year, Palmer teamed with Curtis Fuller and created "FATE Magazine," which is still being published today, more than 60 years later.

Global Communications/Inner Light Publications offers reprints of nearly all of Shaver's stories from that heady early period, both in "The Hidden World" series and another recent book called "Richard Shaver's Chilling Tales From The Inner Earth," edited by Timothy Green Beckley and William Kern. Also included are some of the original magazine covers, many of which look like quality "pop art" and would be worthy of an art museum or gallery showing.

By the early 1960s, the popularity of the Shaver Mysteries had essentially run its course and Shaver had moved on to something new. In his later years, Shaver had come to believe that ancient civilizations had used ordinary rocks to "capture their images."

"Just like you can put a lot of information on a computer disk today," explained publisher and writer Timothy Green Beckley, "Shaver believed that they encoded rocks with all kinds of legends and stories from the days of Atlantis and these underground worlds. He thought that everybody should be able to see the pictures and read the information in the rocks just like he was able to. So every week, he would send me a box of rocks through the mail or by UPS, containing all the dirt and worms and everything from his backyard."

ROCKS WITH ABSOLUTELY NO ROLL!

In spite of the frequent rock shipments, which caused young Beckley's non-comprehending parents no small amount of displeasure, the correspondence between him and Shaver continued for some time. A collection of those unpublished letters is and writings from Shaver are included in the aforementioned book, "The Reality of the Inner Earth," the cover of which shows a photo of Shaver superimposed over one of his mystically encoded rocks.

What did Shaver himself have to say about it all? In another new Inner Light - Global Communications release, called "The Smoky God and Other Inner Earth Mysteries," Shaver is quoted as saying of his reading public: "To me, struggling to find an opening out of the morass – no longer just for myself but now for all mankind – the flood of letters I received from other sufferers was a crushing blow, bringing hopeless despair. The caverns were not, I realized now, a localized thing. They extended underneath every area of the Earth. The evidence of their activity and strength piled up, until I could not help but conclude that there is no answer for present-day man. He cannot break their power over him, nor remedy the ills they visit upon him."

Shaver also writes in a similar pessimistic way about the UFOs, which first received worldwide attention with Kenneth Arnold's sighting in 1947, a few brief years after the publication of "I Remember Lemuria."

"The visits of the saucers," Shaver writes, "bring with them, for me, fresh despair. For I see them as proof of the caverns' contact with space. Knowing the cave people, I know that if any of the visiting saucers were benevolent visitors bringing gifts and knowledge to the surface people, they would be destroyed. To me, that explains the failure to contact our surface government, because those saucers that are not destroyed are our ancient enemies."

What Shaver is talking about is something similar to a concept first put forth by the late alien abduction researcher Budd Hopkins. Hopkins coined the phrase "confirmation anxiety" to describe what happens when an abductee finds proof of the reality of his experiences, such as seeing a mark left behind on his body after recalling that a skin sample had been taken during an abduction episode. A person needs to have some part of his mind in a state of doubt to function as a hiding place where he can call what he has experienced "unreal." When something happens to drive the troublesome memory into a place where the abductee cannot deny that something frightening and strange has really happened to him after all, when his "dreams" are confirmed for him, a whole new kind of anxiety kicks in.

Richard Shaver's death in November 1975 is also fraught with strange happenings. One of his followers and friends, a woman named Mary Jane Martin, knew him at the end. She said that his death was highly suspect, coming on the heels of his having just signed a contract to go to Hollywood and serve as a consultant on a movie about the deros and their Inner Earth kingdom of horror and shame. Shaver was very excited and had even bought new dentures for the occasion. Suddenly, he developed locked bowels and had to be hospitalized. He told his wife that the deros were trying to prevent his cinematic success and he would die there in the hospital. She assured him the operation was not a serious one and he would be fine.

Shaver's wife was quite correct and the surgery did go well. But as he lay recovering, Shaver suffered a pair of small heart attacks.

"Neither of which should have killed him," Martin said, "but he died in that hospital. His prediction came true. The Dero would not let him live to make that movie."

But of course there remains an audience eager to know about the mysteries that so burdened Shaver. Timothy Beckley of Global Communications has made a sort of cottage industry out of interest in the Inner and Hollow Earth theories, saving some old and rare books from obscurity and publishing up-to-date compendiums written by more recent researchers.

And so it is left to us, decades after the deaths of Shaver and Palmer, to try to pick up the pieces and understand Shaver's torture in ways that can help us to deal with the very vocal evils of our own time. The ambitious reprinting efforts by Global Communications/Inner Light Books are an enormous help in those terms and well worth the effort involved in purchasing and reading the writings of a pioneer who seems at times to be whistling in the dark in a benighted, infernal hell, along with the rest of us.

SUGGESTED READING

RICHARD SHAVER: REALITY OF THE INNER EARTH by Tim R. Swartz

THE SMOKY GOD AND OTHER INNER EARTH MYSTERIES: EXPANDED EDITION

RICHARD SHAVER: CHILLING TALES FROM THE INNER EARTH

THE HIDDEN WORLD VOLUME 1: THE DERO! THE TERO! THE BATTLE BETWEEN GOOD AND EVIL UNDERGROUND

14

THE HOLLOW EARTH HASSLE OF MARY JANE MARTIN
By Sean Casteel

She put her very heart and soul into her work. Mary Martin, over a span of several years, published thirteen issues of a very special publication composed of letters and published articles from fans of the Hollow Earth and the Shaver Mystery. As publisher of the "Hollow Hassle" she knew everyone in the Shaver-Hollow Earth field, a field that was small and limited due to its frankly bizarre nature.

Mary, who passed away peacefully in her sleep on November 10, 2016, was the last of the Richard Shaver "inner circle." As probably the most prolific publisher of Inner Earth material today, the editorial staff of this book felt it important that we work with her in putting some of this valuable material together into a practical framework so that it might be available to other students of these remarkable subjects for years to come. Thus our large format trade paperback anthology consisting of the best news items and stories published in her long-defunct newsletter.

Of the original participants in the drama that came to be known as the Shaver Mysteries, very few remain alive today. Both Richard Shaver and his mentor, Raymond Palmer, passed away in 1975, each of them steadfastly maintaining that the work they had published about the Tero and Dero of the Hollow Earth was factual, though its heyday with diehard believers had long since passed.

Among the handful of believers who have kept the subject of the Shaver Mysteries alive and "out there," it was left to Mary Jane to begin publishing a newsletter in the early 1970s devoted to the latest findings about the dark kingdom below our feet that sends such endless misery to us hapless mortals on the surface.

We spoke to Mary Jane and asked how she first came to the subject. She said it all started when she saw an ad for "The Smoky God, Or A Voyage To The Inner World," a 1908 novel by Willis George Emerson which is presented as a true account of a Norwegian sailor who sailed through an entrance to the Earth's interior at the North Pole.

JOINT FORCES
Future Combat Systems Training Area

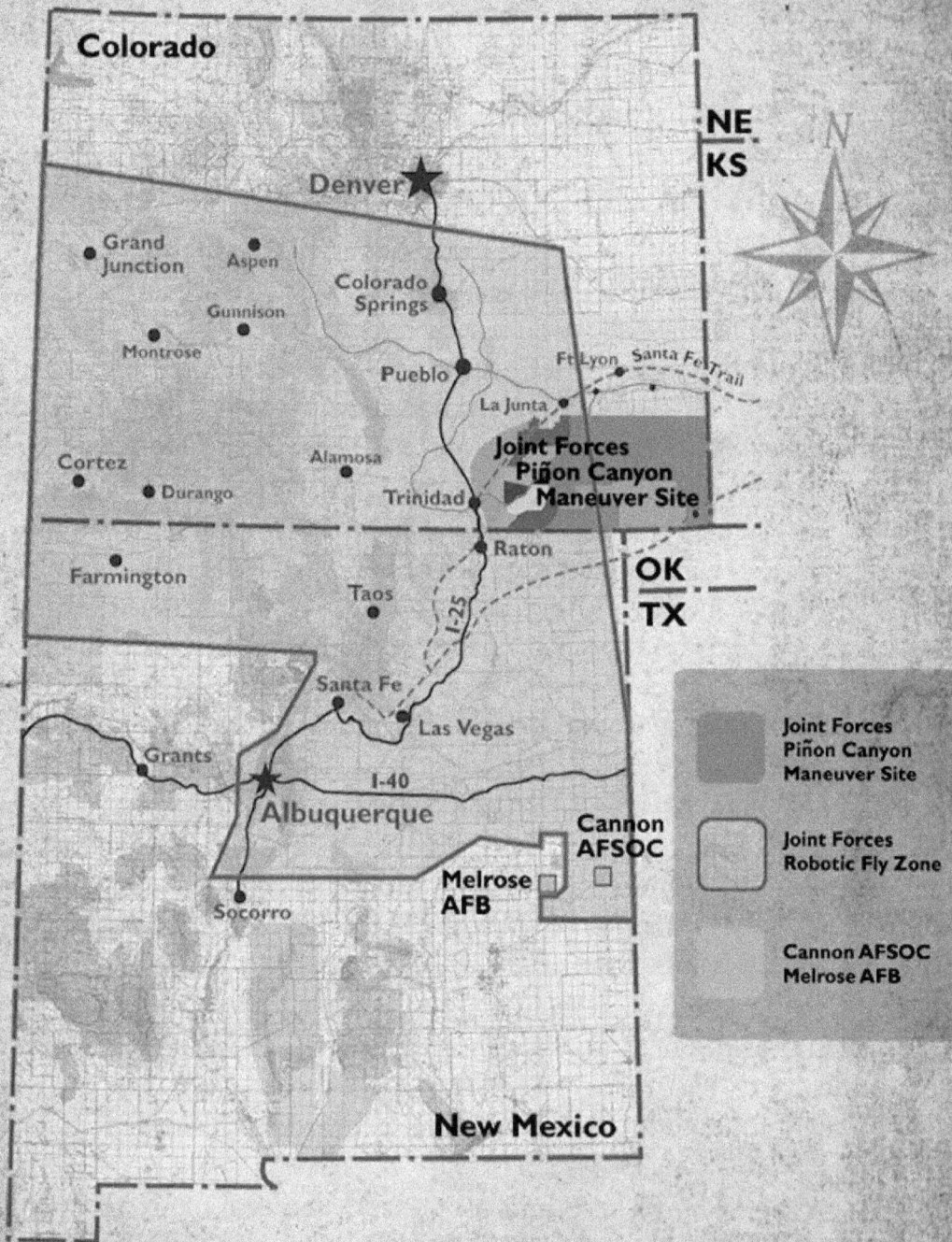

Colorado

NE
KS

Denver

Grand Junction

Aspen

Colorado Springs

Gunnison

Montrose

Ft. Lyon   Santa Fe Trail

Pueblo

La Junta

Cortez

Alamosa

Joint Forces
Piñon Canyon
Maneuver Site

Durango

Trinidad

Raton

OK
TX

Farmington

Taos

I-25

Santa Fe

Las Vegas

Grants

I-40

Albuquerque

Cannon
AFSOC

Melrose
AFB

Joint Forces
Piñon Canyon
Maneuver Site

Joint Forces
Robotic Fly Zone

Cannon AFSOC
Melrose AFB

Socorro

New Mexico

Piñon Canyon Maneuver Site, Colorado - Cannon AFSOC, New Mexico

© Grassland Trust and Not 1 More Acre! • PO Box 773 • Trinidad, Colorado 81082
www.not1moreacre.net • www.grasslandtrust.org

* SECURITY UNIFORM

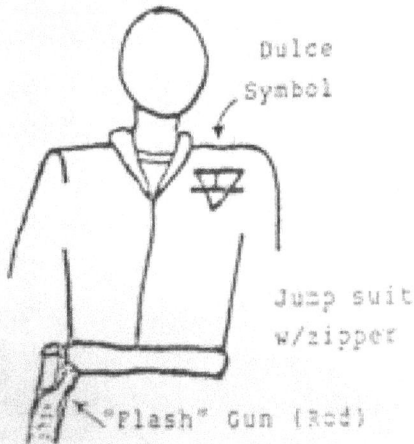

Dulce Symbol

Jump suit w/zipper

"Flash" Gun (Red)

* CODED ELEVATOR CONTROLS

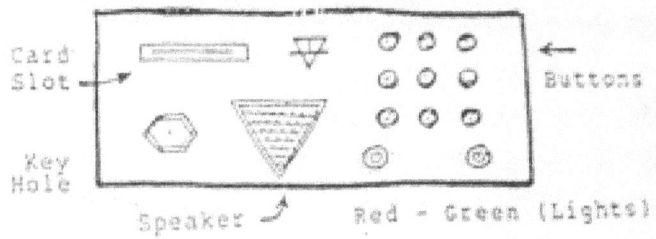

Card Slot →

Key Hole

Buttons ←

Speaker

Red - Green (Lights)

* ELEVATOR & DOOR "ID" CARD

NAME

Dulce Symbol

Code #

Dept #

Vats, similar to the vats at Dulce Base

Surviving witnesses claim that aliens are brought to term in special vats after having been deposited as eggs by the other-worlders.

Cherry Hinkle

MAKING THE VATS AT DULCE BASE?!

Above: Mary Martin and Cherry Hinkle. Below: Mary and TAL

"I can't recall what the ad said," Mary Jane said, "or what piqued my interest enough to send for it, but I have never regretted that I did. This was my first encounter with the theory of a Hollow Earth. I was also receiving a newsletter put out by Dorothy Starr, with its main interest being in the possibility of a polar shift. I wrote to Dorothy and asked her if any of her readers were interested in the theory of a Hollow Earth. She had one member who shared my interest, namely Tom LeVesque, who I started to correspond with."

It was around that time that Mary Jane began printing her own small newsletter called "The Hollow Hassle." LeVesque became her coeditor, and the newsletter was published monthly for a total of thirteen issues. Mary Jane and LeVesque were married in 1973, and began to travel around the country investigating paranormal phenomena, including cattle mutilations.

Mary Jane said that in the wake of reading "The Smoky God" and another book called "Etidorhpa" (an 1898 novel by John Uri Lloyd about a Freemason who descends to the Inner Earth through a cave in Kentucky and encounters strange forms of life there), she knew that solid, real-world information to back up the claims of Shaver and others would be hard to come by. "I knew that it would be a 'hassle' to find any information on this," she explained, "thus the title 'The Hollow Hassle.'"

Due to their travel schedule and dwindling funds, publication of the newsletter ceased for a time. After she and LeVesque separated in 1981, Mary Jane began to print the newsletter again as a quarterly, running for about another seventeen issues into the mid-1980s. It was a gut feeling about Richard Shaver's writings that kept her believing for so long. "There was a lot of factual evidence to show that a Hollow Earth had a good possibility of being true," she said. "Many people are more versed in the scientific aspects than I am, but you do have things like the Narwhales that travel north and disappear. Many legends talk of their ancestors disappearing further north, possibly entering through the North Pole entrance, just as the Narwhales probably are."

Along the way, Mary Jane struck up a relationship with Shaver himself.

"Initially," she said, "I started to correspond [by regular mail] with Dick Shaver, but I did go to his Arkansas home twice. The first time, he looked healthy, but the second visit Dick looked thinner and worn down. I also did a radio talk show interview with Dick, on the Hilly Rose Show. Tom and I did the first show by ourselves, and on the next show, Dick came in at about the halfway mark."

Mary Jane also came to know others who were likewise in pursuit of the truth about the Shaver Mysteries. "I was very fortunate to be in touch with a number of very interesting people," she said. "They included Richard Toronto, of Shavertron fame, Charles Marcoux, who died on the way to Blowing Cave in Arkansas, Joan O'Connell from 'The New Atlantean Journal,' and Bruce Walton, now known as 'Branton,' who was an excellent researcher on the Hollow Earth/Inner Earth."

Did Mary Jane ever do any exploring of caves herself?

"I have explored some caves," she replied, "and I also went to a number of tourist caves. Unfortunately, I did not find a tunnel that led to the Inner Earth, but many of the tourist caves have areas where you are not allowed to go, so who knows how far those areas go? I do feel that the Mammoth Cave in Kentucky may be an entrance."

That there is something wicked lurking in the hollow places is accepted without question by Mary Jane.

"I do believe there is evil in those caves," she said, "and Richard Shaver warned us not to go into the caves. There are too many crazy things that happen on Earth, with no apparent reason for them to happen. One man got hit by lightning twice in his life. What are the odds of that? Young people do things that are very evil and they seem to have no control over their actions. Deros would explain a lot of things. Also, when Ray Palmer stayed overnight at Richard's house, he heard voices."

Still, a certain amount of controversy continues to enshroud the relationship of Shaver and Palmer and the literal truth as understood between them. For example, Palmer once declared that during the time Shaver was allegedly underground, Shaver was instead in a mental institution in a coma. We asked Mary Jane for her thoughts on the controversy. "That's a tough question," she said. "A lot of people think it was an astral trip that Richard took while being in a coma, and that may be. But whether it's an actual trip or an astral one, on some level it is real. It certainly was to Richard, and I'm inclined to believe him. We got pretty close in the years that we knew each other.

"I feel that Richard wrote what he believed to be true," Mary Jane continued, "and then Palmer dressed it up to make it more exciting and saleable. Palmer only paid Richard one and a half cents per word, and I think there was trouble about that."

Much of the unhappy events that have transpired in the years since Mary Jane blames quite firmly on the Dero, including her own health problems, among other things.

"At one time," she said, "I do think they were stopping me from putting out 'The Hollow Hassle,' as I had been rushed to the hospital twice with chest pains. It wasn't just me that was being hit by the Deros. Joan O'Connell, who had published more Hollow Earth info, died from a heart attack. She had no heart problems previously. Then her material went to Gray Barker, who was going to continue publishing her newsletter. He died three months after Joan, from a heart attack, I believe. Then Charles Marcoux was killed by a number of bees as he was heading towards Blowing Cave in Arkansas."

But nothing tops the death of Richard Shaver himself when it comes to strange factors being at play. "Richard Shaver's death was highly suspect also," Mary Jane said. "He had signed a contract to come to Hollywood and be a consultant on a movie about the Tero and Dero. He was very excited and even got new dentures for the occasion. Then he came down with locked bowels and had to go into the hospital. He told his wife Dot that the Dero would not let him make this movie and he would die in the hospital. She assured him that it was not a serious operation and that he would be fine."

Dot was quite correct that the surgery itself would go well. But as he lay recovering in his hospital bed, Shaver suffered a pair of small heart attacks. "Neither of which should have killed him," Mary Jane said, "but he died in that hospital. His prediction came true. The Dero would not let him live to make that movie. Afterwards, Dot could not find the contract for the movie or who was making it, as we wanted to check into that further."

Finally, Mary Jane said the Hollow Earth may have been created initially as the Garden of Eden, despite the scoffing of modern day science. "Science is wrong a lot," she said, "and they still don't really know much about what is below our feet. Someone told me that if God was going to build a house for Adam and Eve, would he build it so they had to live on the porch outside the house, or would he build it where there was no glaring sun, with large gardens of fruit, stable temperatures, etc., such as the Hollow Earth? Perhaps when Adam and Eve got thrown out of the Garden, it meant that they were tossed out of the Inner World, to suffer the extreme climates on the outside of the Earth."

Were we indeed cast out of an Inner Earth paradise when we fell from grace? Like so much of the Shaver Mysteries to which Mary Jane has devoted years of study, the answer may lie in some hidden place that only Richard Shaver and a few others have ever reached. In any case, we are left to struggle against the Dero ourselves, or whatever the embodiment of evil that still tortures mankind is ultimately called. And Mary Jane's place in that overall scheme of things can be read right here, in the pages of yet another attempt to make sense of the unknowable before it is too late to make sense of anything.

SUGGESTED READING

HOLLOW EARTH HASSLE by Mary Martin

www.Facebook.com/ShavertronPress

Surveyor's mark indicates the location of Mount Tipton.

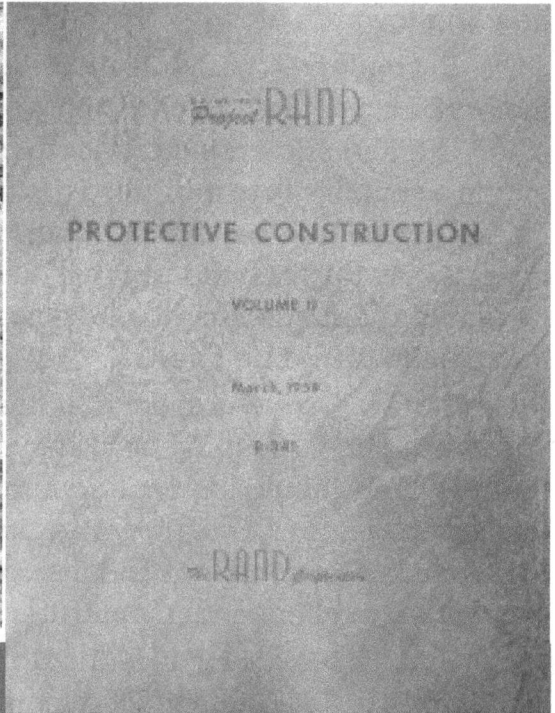

PROTECTIVE CONSTRUCTION

VOLUME II

March, 1958

RAND

People and locations associated with the secret entrance to the Inner World near Mount Tipton.

TAL   John Rhodes   Ruben Uriarte

SECRET EXPLOITS OF ADMIRAL RICHARD E. BYRD
MORE CHILLING TALES OF THE SHAVER MYSTERY AND THE INNER EARTH

MEN IN BLACK, UFOS AND UNDERGROUND CITIES NEAR HOPLAND, CALIFORNIA

It seems like a lot of "strange things" happen out of town along isolated trails and deep back in the woods where city folk seldom venture. A lot has been made about the perplexing paranormal and UFO related incidents associated with the Skinwalker Ranch in Utah and Marley Woods deep in the thickets of Missouri. You can read up on this in George Knapp's book and watch our interview on YouTube with physical trace case investigator Ted Phillips.

* * * * *

"Sirs... The thing that I am trying to say is that I think I can show you an entrance to this subterranean city that he has written about several issues back.

"Here is what happened to me and you may judge for yourself. In 1931 my mother and I took up this section of land as a cattle raising homestead from the U.S. Government, and naturally it was not a choice piece. First of all, no one before us was able to locate the land even with the assistance of maps and the land office, but we are friendly people, so a person who turned out to be our nearest neighbor gave us some hints. And, as the place was only six miles from his, we stayed at his ranch until we built our house. Then we moved into our own and all in all we stayed there about two years before we quit...

"There are too many incidents to be told in one letter. The best one was the disappearing automobiles, which happened about ten at night over at the neighbor's place. It was as follows: the neighbor and we were sitting on the porch after supper, when he saw headlights come over the hill to the fence then along the fence for about half a mile, then go out and that was all that night. So next morning we went to the trail along the fence, and there were tire tracks of seven inch width tires going along the fence into the box canyon and right up against a smooth boulder about 20 feet in diameter and ended there. Now the car could not turn around anywhere in that place because the road is a trail five feet wide and one side is against our neighbor's fence, which was not damaged and the other was a steep hill that no car could even make in compound low. You know, we have a few mountains here, and as far as backing out I tried that myself in the daytime with help, but I could not steer a straight enough path without crossing my other marks so they did not back out or we would have trailed them as my neighbor has lived around there since 1848 and he sure knew his tracking. We never did get an answer to the question of where did the cars go.

"The cars were very large and black (Note: Such cars have often been seen by UFO witnesses being driven by the so-called Men In Black who often intimidate such witnesses and tell them to remain silent... suggesting that there is a definite subterranean aspect to not only the UFO phenomena, but also to the 'Men In Black' mystery as well) and very heavy. Now that I compare them they were about twenty years ahead of anything I had ever seen anywhere, and I had worked in the auto business for about five years before we took up that land. They were silent, smooth, no wavering of the lights and the trail is extremely rough; in places it has hollows a yard deep, but these cars went through at about 25 mph. I would even wreck a jeep to do that, so you figure it out and let me know the answer if you can. By wavering the lights, I mean that the beams were steady and not flashing up and down as an ordinary car would do when a rough road is traveled.

"I have been away from there since 1933, but just about three months ago, I drove through with a friend for safety and my place was razed to the ground with everything that was made by human hands carried off, even the old tin cans, and that place would not be noticed unless you knew where it was.

The Coast and Geodetic survey had a marker near my house in the front yard and even that was gone; who would want to take a concrete marker and carry it away? Don't tell me about the lumber shortage, as this place is near lumber camps and mills; and other abandoned houses still stand in the valley, but they are thirty miles away and safe from the things. By near lumber, I mean within 50 miles radius.

"Characteristics of the vicinity are one: no wind; two: silence. You can hear your heart beat and after two weeks, you can hear insects running on the ground; three: Forest fires will not burn there. They burnt 250,000 acres, then burnt all around this area; and that stopped the forest rangers. They could never understand because most of it is on the slope of a mountain and it should have gone, but they say that the wind came down and blew from the top down and blew North, South, East and West at once. That was the only time that the wind ever blew there...

"It is located 110 miles north of San Francisco in Mendocino County, directly on the old Pieta toll road that runs between Hopland and Lakeport in Lake County, of which Clear Lake is quite a summer resort. If you care to look it up on a map, get a good auto road map and look due south off the road midway between towns, and you will note an area with no roads bounded by Sonoma Lake and the lower Mendocino counties and there it is. If you wish to go there, be sure that enough people know where you went. Maybe they will be able to find you. There have been several disappearances along that stretch of road, even trucks have vanished. All the U.S. Government's.

"The U.S. Government has noted the area as rough, unsurvey-able and UNEXPLORED. Before you visit the area, please let me know and I will assist you every way possible, but don't take any unnecessary chances if you do. I have a '41 Dodge and I could not make the road to my neighbor's ranch. The car would not make the turns and the engine did not have enough power to pull the hill, so I do not know as to whether he is alive or not. I inquired at the nearest habitation about 15 miles, and they did not know him, as they have only been there six months, so I am none the wiser...

"I have tried to interest many people to investigate this, but even the government is helpless as you well know, as far as this goes. Also I forgot to mention there is a cave on the property that has steps leading down and there is no sound when a rock is thrown in. I have never seen it, but I understand that it is there. To give you an idea, if you leave the road 100 yards, it takes two minutes and it will take you two hours to climb back 100 yards...

"Since I left the ranch I have been in the radio business... Also not changing the subject, but I have run across a person who is not from this earth, and while I can't get him to admit it, I have found evidence that point to the fact that he came here from a planet that has tropics and a polar ice cap next to each other with no temperate zone. He knows radio perfectly, but earns his living by going to sea as a desk officer, and someday I will trip him up and get him to admit it, but up to now I have had very little success.

"Hoping to hear from you if possible, and if you print this, okay, but no help for curious public. But if you know of someone capable in the vicinity, have them get in touch with me and I will give more details."

— Edward John., 475 Fell Street, San Francisco 2, Calif.

Letter courtesy Olav Philips and Paranoia magazine.

www.ParanoiaMagazine.com

SUGGESTED READING

Hunt For The Skinwalker, by George Knapp

UFO Silencers: Mystery Of The Men In Black by Tim Beckley

They Knew Too Much About Flying Saucers by Gray Barker

* * * * *

THE BLOWING CAVES AND THE SHAVER MYSTERY

One of the odd stories related to Inner Earth is set in Blowing Cave, near Cushman, Arkansas, where a man named George D. Wight is said to have found a subterranean civilization and proven the Shaver Mystery. Though Wight disappeared, his story survives in a diary he allegedly wrote. In the 1950s, Wight was a UFO buff from Michigan. Wight knew of Richard Shaver's claims, published in the 1940s in the Ziff-Davis science-fiction magazines Amazing Stories and Fantastic Adventures, that the remnants of two advanced races, Tero and Dero (good and evil respectively), lived in vast caverns under Earth's surface.

Though Wight was skeptical of these claims, he had an interest in cave-exploring that he indulged with David L., for whose mimeographed saucer newsletter Wight contributed a regular column.

They did their spelunking with three other men. All of them were acquainted with Charles A. Marcoux, another columnist for the magazine. Unlike the others, Marcoux was an obsessed believer in Shaverian concepts, to the extent that he gave occasional public lectures on the subject. The spelunkers sometimes attended those lectures but considered his beliefs absurd.

In 1966 the group, now consisting of twelve persons, went down to Arkansas to explore Blowing Cave on a week-long expedition. On their return, members wrote letters to Ray Palmer, once editor of Amazing Stories and Shaver's principal promoter, claiming that they had encountered intelligent beings – Shaver's Tero – deep inside the cavern. Palmer did not reply. Apparently a few months later, Wight went back and chose to stay with the under-earth people. He returned in 1967 to give a written account to David L., who by this time had left the UFO field and no longer wanted to be publicly associated with it. Wight asked L. to pass on the diary to Charles Marcoux. Wight felt that in ridiculing his beliefs he had wronged him and wanted to provide him with the proof that Shaver was right.

He then returned to his Tero friends and has not been seen since. David L., however, had long since lost track of Marcoux, and it was not until thirteen years later that he came upon his name. He tracked him down and handed him the manuscript. Its effect on Marcoux was electrifying, and it set in motion the events that would eventually lead to his premature death.

The manuscript related that while exploring Blowing Cave, the group spotted a light at the end of a tunnel. As the spelunkers approached it, Wight noticed a narrow crevice, just big enough for him to squeeze inside it. There he found clearly artificial steps. He called to his friends, and they climbed through the opening. On the other side of it, the opening expanded, and they were able to walk upright. "Suddenly," Wight wrote, "we came into a large tunnel/corridor, about twenty feet wide and just as high. All the walls and the floor were smooth, and the ceiling had a curved dome shape. We knew that this was not a freak of nature, but man made. We had accidentally stumbled into the secret cavern world"

Soon they encountered blue-skinned but otherwise human like individuals. The strangers said that they had permitted the crew to find the tunnel and enter it, because they had instruments that measured people's emotions; the explorers were determined to have good intentions.

They learned that the tunnels went on for hundreds of miles and led to under earth cities populated by entities that included serpent-like creatures and Sasquatch-like hairy bipeds. Soon after their initial conversation, Wight and his companions were taken to a kind of elevator that led them to the under earthers' place of residence, a city made of glass.

SECRET EXPLOITS OF ADMIRAL RICHARD E. BYRD

It turned out that their guides were Noah's direct descendants, who had found their way underground in the wake of the flood. There they found super technology and the remains of an advanced civilization, along with Tero. Apparently at some point, Wight's group met the Tero who had been there all along.

This was not the only trip the group took to Blowing Cave. Unable to get anybody on the surface to believe their story, Wight and his friends vowed to return with conclusive proof. During one expedition, they captured a giant cave moth, preserved it in a bag, and brought it up with them. When they opened the bag, however, the sunlight disintegrated the insect into a fine dust.

Not long afterward, Wight decided to stay with the under earth people. According to one source, "all evidence of [his] ever existing began to mysteriously disappear from the surface. Birth certificates, school records, computer records, bank records, etc., all seemed to vanish, apparently the work of someone in a very influential position"

Other members of the group made another trip into the cave, where they saw their friend for the last time. Wight returned once to the surface to meet David L. In 1980, Marcoux saw the manuscript and read Wight's words addressed to him: "Yes, Charles, all that you told us is true. . . I owe you a debt of gratitude, because the Tero healed my crippled leg, instantly. I am grateful for more than just that, and I have left these notes and somewhere a map so that you, too, can . . . visit with these people. . . . Maybe we will meet here someday"

Marcoux set about organizing an expedition, 46 Blowing Cave, soliciting members in such small-circulation Hollow-Earth publications as Shavertron and The Hollow Hassle. Marcoux and his wife moved to Cushman in 1983. There, in November, as he was visiting the land around the cave, a swarm of bees descended on him. The resulting shock and trauma precipitated a heart attack, and he died on the spot.

Some Hollow-Earth enthusiasts speculated that sinister forces that wanted to keep the caves a secret had caused the attack. Others saw it as just a tragic accident. In any case, Marcoux's death ended efforts to explore Blowing Cave in search of under-earthers.

www.AstraFreaks.net

PUBLISHER BECKLEY JOINS IN

Never one to be kept out of participating in the conversation, publisher/ editor Tim Beckley felt a need to give a few of his own qualifications for issuing this latest volume in well over a dozen books he has published on the Inner and Hollow Earth theories, and in particular his fascination with what Richard Shaver had to say over the years since Palmer first ran the presses of "Amazing Stories" overtime in the mid-1040s. The web site "Conspiracy Archive" published some years ago an extensive interview with Beckley. He has "watered it down" somewhat to fit space limitations. The interview was conducted by Terry Melanson.

ConspiracyArchive: So tell us about your relationship to Richard Shaver.

Timothy Beckley: Well, of course, for many years Shaver was part and parcel of almost everything Palmer did in the field. Shaver and I corresponded. I would get a letter from him every few days. Not very well written and on a typewriter that had not had its ribbon changed in years it seemed. I was 16 years old I think and Shaver would send me a box of his picture rocks like clockwork every week or so. My mother dreaded the arrival of the box as the rocks were right out of Shaver's yard. The box was filled with dirt and worms and God knows what.

Shaver, Palmer and I had a lively debate going for a while over the reality of the subsurface world. I put a lot of this material together into a book that was published by Gray Barker's long since defunct Saucerian Press. "47?_encoding=UTF8&camp=1789&link_code=xm2"The Shaver Mystery and The Inner Earth" went through several printings. By the time I was 17 my career as a writer was etched in stone, I guess you could say...even though I had just about failed English in high school. Today our companies Inner Light and Global Communications have about 85 titles in print by authors like Commander X, Brad Steiger, Tim Swartz, T. Lobsang Rampa. A bootleg edition of "The Shaver Mystery" is sold on the net by Health Research. Have never seen a cent on it so if you want the full story get my book "Subterranean Worlds Inside Earth," which has all this original material plus a lot more. It is available from Amazon or from our own website www.conspiracyjournal.com

ConspiracyArchive: Most "UFO researchers" today might consider the Hollow Earth theory a "crackpot" subject, but since the beginnings of the modern UFO sightings it has been intimately connected with "UFOlogy" — especially early contactees. Why do you think this has been forgotten?

Timothy Beckley: Unlike most folks who consider themselves UFO researchers and paranormal investigators, I have never had a deep set belief pattern. Some UFOs may be interplanetary craft, but the majority have to be placed in some other category. During radio and TV interviews, the host will always ask what is MY opinion about UFOs. I always tell him it doesn't matter what my opinion is — as UFOs act independently of my beliefs or anyone else's!

What really got me thinking about this Inner Earth stuff was back years ago there were three miners trapped in a cave in Pennsylvania. It was all over the newspapers and radio back then. They were not expected to survive after three or four days of not being heard from. They were eventually rescued. In the hospital, the miners said that after about two days or so they saw an eerie light in the cavern where they were trapped. They followed it and came across a door that led to beings who gave them food and water so they were able to stay alive.

There are so many legends that tell about miners trapped in caves who have experiences with a race of short beings. To this day I don't know if Shaver was simply repeating these stories that he could have heard, or if he was really in touch with these Tero and Dero. Shaver's writings were titillating and well written. Palmer probably jazzed them up as I never found Shaver to be a very good writer. Palmer was a real pro. Some say he was responsible for starting the flying saucer mystery with the Maury Island "hoax." If anything, he did keep the mystery alive during its lean years. We need a few more Palmers in the field today. I'm afraid today's breed of self-professed "experts" are a wee bit boring!

I'm afraid I am a bit of a fence-setter. All this could be real or none of it could be! But we should investigate such matters. Beats watching TV 18 hours a day.

Actually, I am a bit more predisposed to believe in the Shaver Mystery rather than accept the idea of openings at the North and South Poles. Not totally convinced of this theory yet. Want to see more proof.

And while Shaver and Palmer are long gone from our realm, their spirits definitely live on. There is still a great deal of interest in what they wrote, and a whole new generation that wants to be exposed to what they had to offer the world. If I have my way, I will continue to be a source for what they had to say!

ConspiracyArchive: You related some good miners stories in your book as well. This is one of the most convincing parts of it in my mind. Someone should go out and interview a bunch of them. Has anyone compiled a book strictly on the tales of miners in the tunnels?

Timothy Beckley: As far as I know there has not been an attempt to compile all the stories that miners have told about strange things happening underground. But in my various writings I do quote from some of the sources that are known to me.

The well-known conspiracy author Branton (who once wrote an index to the Inner Earth under his real name Bruce Walton for Saucerian Press) has quite a bit of this information on his various web sites.

By the way, I just got word that Branton was in a very serious accident. Apparently he was riding his bicycle when a truck plowed in to him. He is, at last word, in intensive care — but I don't have the information as to what hospital he might be in.

We could use a few active researchers to explore the old journals and books for more exploits by miners and cave explorers. There is probably a ton of uncovered material out there just waiting to be discovered. Unfortunately, we don't have someone with the influence like Ray Palmer — or his magazines — to attract attention or "get the word out." I bet there are all kinds of small circulation publications put out by amateur cave explorers that would provide us with lots of new stories.

ConspiracyArchive: In India popular belief has it that tunnel entrances are guarded by elementals. Kirk of Aberfoyle in the 1600s wrote of the cave dwellers with similar occult overtones. What's your take on these theories?

Timothy Beckley: Almost every country has its stories. India is no different. Many, many years ago Dr. Robert Dickhoff used to write about some of these matters. He did the book "Homecoming of the Martians," which gave very sinister overtones to the UFO mystery. In many legends, the entrances to the caves were guarded by the Genies — who somehow later ended up in a bottle that you could rub three times and have your wish come true.

ConspiracyArchive: I know you've managed to take a photograph of one of the Men in Black. This is said to be the only one in existence. Maybe you could tell us how that came about and what if any is the relation of the MIBs to Inner Earth Traditions?

Timothy Beckley: I was with Jim Moseley when we took the photo of this MIB. He was standing in a doorway in Jersey City dressed all in black just like Albert K. Bender had described in Barker's "They Knew Too Much" book.

This MIB was standing directly across the street from the apartment building where ve.com/UFOs/tunnels.html"Jack Robinson lived. Jack was a freelance editor on the staff of Jim Moseley's *Saucer News*.

Jack had collected a lot of Shaver material. In fact, in my book, "Subterranean Worlds Inside Earth," he tells the story of a Steve Brodie who lived in the same apartment complex as Jack and his wife Mary (NOT the one where the MIB was sighted standing near). Brodie was a hermit of sorts who had no friends. Jack ran into him in the hallway one day and Steve invited him into his apartment where he proceeded to tell him of an experience out west that involved being in a cave and seeing creatures like what Shaver had claimed existed. Brodie was last seen on a train in Arizona looking like he was in a trance....and as if he were returning to where he had this encounter with the Dero.

Jack told the story numerous times on the Long John Nebel show and wrote quite a bit on the Inner Earth for my newsletter "The Searchlight." Bender always talked about UFO bases at the South Pole. So there is a definite connection here. I can't say for sure who this character was that Jim and I photographed. But the picture is published in my book "glance&s=books"The UFO Silencers: Mystery of the Men in Black."

ConspiracyArchive: Some of the amazing discoveries of Tesla and John Keel bear a strong similarity to Shaver's descriptions of the Deros' "mech-ray" technology. Did you ever talk to Shaver about these inventions?

Timothy Beckley: Unfortunately, in the last days of his life, Shaver didn't seem to want to talk about the Dero and the Tero or their mech rays technology — and I was not that knowledgeable about Tesla in those days (remember I was only 16 or 17 years old when I corresponded with Shaver). By that time he was pretty much into his rock phase. I was interested in the rocks but you have to have a bit of patience to work with them.

By the way, I don't recall if I mentioned it or not, but I purchased the last 50 copies of "The Secret World" that Palmer and Shaver did together on the rock phenomenon. Its available either directly from our website or you can order it off of Amazon. Toward the end, Shaver had a very bitter attitude toward most people, as he felt he has been used to a large extent, in that people only heard what they wanted to hear and believe what they wanted to believe. Shaver believed in a physical world beneath our feet. No astral projections, no ghosts, no demons. Pure and simple Dero and Tero without the frills.

Who else is really writing about subject and not rehashing material? I would like to do an update on the Shaver mystery and the Inner Earth. A lot of my material was ruined in a flood a couple of years ago. I would like to get some of the better letters and stories from early Shaver and Palmer magazines if anyone has anything to lend, donate or email. Firsthand or passed down accounts also would be welcome. Anyone reading this can always email me at mrufo8@hotmail.com and maybe we can put together something in the next year or two. Anyone contributing material will receive a free copy and credit.

SUGGESTED READING – BOOKS WRITTEN OR CO-AUTHORED BY TIMO-THY G BECKLEY

AMITYVILLE AND BEYOND

NAZI UFO TIME TRAVELERS

UFO REPEATERS: THE CAMERA DOESN'T LIE

SECRETS OF DEATH VALLEY

PROJECT ALIEN MIND CONTROL

ROUND TRIP TO HELL IN A FLYING SAUCER

www.ConspiracyJournal.com (email mrufo8@hotmail for free printed edition)

ALL THAT GLITTERS: A FEW ADDED COMMENTS
BY TIM BECKLEY

Trust me when I tell you that all the stories and folklore about our "paradise" inside the Earth do NOT go far enough in their attempts to lay down the facts about this world within a world. There are many dangers beneath our surface, says California researcher Richard Toronto.

And Richard Toronto should know because Richard Toronto is a certified voyeur.

He has been spying on at least two individuals for more than a decade and he undoubtedly has the scoop on everything they have ever done and said.

Rich is a fan of the Shaver Mystery. He has a vast collection of memorabilia

Richard Toronto makes a rare appearance on the show "Exploring The Bizarre," hosted by Tim Beckley and Tim Swartz.

attesting to this fact. He knows everything there is to know about Richard S. Shaver and the underworld denizens called the Dero, as well as the late publisher/editor/theorist Raymond A Palmer (RAP for short) who first published Shaver's stories in a sci-fi journal published during the mid-1940s. "Amazing Stories" had a solid readership for a pulp magazine. But when Shaver's tales were added to the digest, circulation increased two-fold as many readers added their two cents worth proclaiming that Shaver was right, that they had also heard voices – voices that told them to do terrible things from killing, committing arson, fostering wars and global conflict.

Shaver said this inner world was ancient. That this conflict had been going on since time immemorial. That the Dero had the use of weird telepathic machinery by which they could control our thoughts and command us to do dastardly deeds against our will.

Toronto follows Shaver and Palmer home from the publishers' office and takes a peek into their private lives. The Air Force once said Ray Palmer "created" the flying saucer mystery, which may be an over-simplification, but he did hire Kenneth Arnold, the "first" flying saucer observer, to track down rumors of a crashed UFO, only to have a run-in with sinister forces who seemed to know what he was thinking.

SECRET EXPLOITS OF ADMIRAL RICHARD E. BYRD

SHAVEROLOGY – A SHAVER MYSTERY HOME COMPANION is a must read for those who thought they knew all there was to know about a subject that has been the center of extreme controversy for many decades.

RICHARD TORONTO, TOMMY KNOCKERS AND SHAVERTRON

Throughout gold mining communities, the seasoned prospectors tell tales of the Tommy Knockers, dwarf-sized beings who lay in wait in the mines and steal the precious metals. They sometimes, I am told, remove it in wheelbarrows if someone has hit the motherlode or just grab a handful of nuggets and flee back from where they came – deep within the Earth. The miners would like to wring the necks of these dastardly punks from "down below," but the Tommy Knockers are known for being slippery gnomes who scatter about in the dark like a pack of rats.

There have even been cases where miners have taken potshots at their mortal enemies, which really puts them in harm's way as it's possible for such a shooting to cause a portion of the mine walls to collapse and injure or trap an individual.

So beware of the Tommy Knockers – or read up on them in Stephen King's bestselling novel, which takes the same name.

And if you don't believe that many dangers exist beneath the surface, just converse with Californian Richard Toronto, who for years has kept the mighty Dero

Striking an amusing pose (we think), Richard Toronto holds the Ten Commandments - perhaps - of the Shaver Mystery

at bay – at least in a literary sense.

With the mighty pen in hand (or a more modernized laptop) and his ear to the (cavern) wall, Toronto has become a certified subterranean voyeur of sorts. In this capacity he has been spying on at least two individuals for more than a decade and he undoubtedly has the scoop on everything they have ever done and said.

In 1972 Richard S. Shaver opened a letter from an inquisitive Golden State kid named Richard Toronto. As the story goes, Shaver's reply changed Toronto's life forever. For the next four years until Shaver's death in 1975, Toronto enrolled in Shaver's rock book correspondence course, where Shaver encouraged him to photograph rocks and become a writer. A few years after Shaver's death, Toronto founded "Shavertron," a fanzine for Shaver Mystery buffs. In time it gathered a cult following, keeping Shaver's memory alive for 29 issues, from 1979 to 1992, as "The Only Source of Post-Deluge Shaverania." It took another 35 years before Toronto wrote the book that became Shaver's first published biography: "War Over Lemuria." Since its publication in 2013, Toronto's California-based Shavertron Press has produced several ground-breaking new works on Shaver and the Mystery. Rokfogo, a two-volume set devoted entirely to Shaver's career of antediluvian rock painting and photography, was the first of its kind.

Over the years Toronto has assembled a huge collection of memorabilia attesting to the fact that he is the world's biggest fan of the Shaver Mystery and knows everything there is to know about Richard S. Shaver and the underworld denizens called the Dero, as well as the late publisher/editor and Hollow Earth theorist Raymond A. Palmer.

As already mentioned, RAP first published Shaver's stories in the sci-fi journal "Amazing Stories" and built a solid readership for the digest-sized newsprint monthly, in an era when print runs were monitored because of a national paper shortage in connection with the war effort.

Shaver confirmed to Rich that that the subterranean foes of humankind, the Dero, were responsible for all sorts of mayhem on the surface, including killing, committing arson, fostering wars and all sorts of global conflict (i.e. they must be really active today it would seem!).

In short, if you think you know about the Shaver Mystery and the Inner Earth, you are unfortunately being deluded unless you go to Richard Toronto's blog on a regular basis and scoop up on the info presented in Shavertron. It just might help keep the Dero at a safe distance and render them powerless.

SECRET EXPLOITS OF ADMIRAL RICHARD E. BYRD

SUGGESTED READING BY RICHARD TORONTO

SHAVEROLOGY: A SHAVER MYSTERY HOME COMPANION

ROCKFOGO: THE MYSTERIOUS PRE-DELUGE ART OF RICHARD SHAVER

SHAVERTRON: THE MIMEOGRAPH YEARS

WAR OVER LEMURIA: RICHARD SHAVER, RAY PALMER AND THE STRANGEST CHAPTER OF 1940s SCIENCE FICTION

"http://www.Shavertron.com" www.Shavertron.com\\

Reptoids, a specific type of serpent race, are in charge of the lower levels of some areas of the Underworld.

TWO OF THE GREATEST MASTER TEACHERS OF OUR TIME INVITE YOU TO VISIT THE CAPITOL OF THE INNER EARTH

JOURNEY WITH DR. RAYMOND BERNARD AND T. LOBSANG RAMPA TO AGHARTA PARADISE? CITY OF ETERNAL YOUTH? A PHYSICAL HELL AT THE PLANET'S CORE?

( ) Man, Beast, Gods of Agharta by Ferdinand Ossendowsky Special Update by Dr Raymond Bernard - $22.00

A lot has been written on the secrets of Tibet as well as the mysteries surrounding the existence of a hollow or inner earth that is said to be teaming with life - huge, unknown, plants, "strange" animals and even human beings. In the mid 1960s Dr. Raymond Bernard shocked the world when he revealed the existence of a inhabited interior or hollow earth which could be entered through various vantage points such as the North and South Poles.

Practically every ancient society had their own tales of magnificent realms, brave heroes and enlightened beings who lived in the inner spheres. Whether people considered the inner world to exist in a spiritual realm or to be an actual physical place, the beliefs, myths and legends all across the globe are all strangely similar. Many Native Americans believe that their ancestors originated from a beautiful subterranean realm, or took refuge in caverns to escape past cataclysms. The Cherokee Indians speak of a subterranean world much like our own, with mountains, rivers, trees, and people.

This work tells in part the journey of the adventurer Ferdinand Ossendowsky who was attempting to escape his native Russia at the height of the communist take over and ends up hearing bizarre tales of Shangri La and the King of the World, who rules over the lost city of Agharta and millions of Buddhists with a wide-reaching, benevolent hand.

Here is his astounding – but TRUE! – story of a grand trip to another realm whose inhabitants wish to keep their kingdom a closely guarded secret from a very aggressive humankind bent on expansionism and conquest.

( ) My Visit To Agharta by T. Lobsang Rampa - $22.00

NEWS FLASH! SECRET LONG LOST MANUSCRIPT FOUND! FOR OVER HALF A CENTURY RAMPA'S FASCINATING NARRATIVES HAVE BROUGHT GREAT JOY AND ENLIGHTENMENT TO MILLIONS WORLDWIDE

Always at the center of controversy, T. Lobsang Rampa initialy came to the attention of the public in the 1950's. *THE THIRD EYE* received wide acclaim by a public that was just beginning to awaken to diverse forms of spirituality.

WHAT MADE RAMPA DIFFERENT from other "teachers," is he did not push any of his experiences down the throats of others, but in a simple, humble fashion, told of a more peaceful, serene life style which had come to him after years of hardship in his homeland. Tibet had been invaded by the Chinese communists, and many monks and adepts had to flee for their lives. But Rampa was able to survive due to deep understanding and application of cosmic laws he had learned from several sources, including masters of the planet Venus, as well as beings from the Inner Earth.

In this just recently released work, Rampa tells of both his positive inner earth contacts and his hellish encounters below the surface where most know nothing about the existence of entire cities and their both angelic and hideous dwellers.

( ) BOTH BOOKS JUST $38.00 (add $5 S/H to order) Ask for AGHARTA TWIN BOOK SPECIAL.

Order From: Timothy Beckley Box 753 · New Brunswick, NJ 08903

SURVEY THE HEIGHTS AND DEPTHS OF MYSTERIOUS MOUNT SHASTA AS YOU READ THE BOOK THAT ALTERED SHIRLEY MACLAINE'S LIFE AND CHARTED THE SPIRITUAL PATHS OF THOUSANDS OF DEVOTED BELIEVERS OVER THE COURSE OF A CENTURY

"DWELLER ON TWO PLANETS" BY PHYLOS REMAINS AT THE HEART OF THE NEW AGE MOVEMENT

Now read our **UPDATED NEW EDITION** - Edited And Grammatically Revised For Easier Comprehension For The Modern Reader By Sean Casteel With New Material Added By Nick Redfern, Timothy Green Beckley And Paul Dale Roberts.

The original **DWELLER ON TWO PLANETS** is said to be one of the most important texts of the 19th Century. For over a hundred years it has been passed around among those seeking the true Spiritual Path to life. Many have said it has impacted them greatly. Actress Shirley MacLaine had little interest in the occult when she was browsing in a Hong Kong bookstore only to have this work literally fall into her hands. It led to many changes in her life and a metaphysical best seller of her own, *Out On A Limb*.

Young author/channel Frederick S. Oliver spins a tale so compelling and so spiritually uplifting that it is doubtful that it was written by him alone as a human being. The reader will immediately see that such a wealth of detail about Atlantis and the spiritual reality could not be conjured from the imagination of an eighteen year old while working as a simple fence mender for his father who raised cattle near their home along the base of the mysterious and legendary Mount Shasta in Northern California.

Oliver foreshadows much of what would come after him, like the feminist movement of the 20th Century, the coming of UFOs with their external multicolored revolving lights and the interiors of the craft lit by some unseen light source, details verified repeatedly by modern day alien abductees and UFO contactees. In fact, many of the illustrations in this book of cigar-shaped craft look remarkably like the ships said to have been photographed by George Adamski and others decades later. Oliver, while in the channeling state, held in the thrall of an Atlantian and ancient Tibetan soul, also predicts television and cell phones in a time that predated even rudimentary radio.

Says Sean Casteel, who updated this major work into modern grammar and phraseology:

"The moral dynamics of the story will hold you spellbound, as the sins of one man's incarnation in Atlantis are repaid in his life as a gold miner in the American West. The story of the latter's initiation into a deeply secret gathering of spiritual adepts and how it leads to adventures in other dimensions will open your eyes to mysteries you never knew existed. . .This book is truly a message from the other side, and contains within it countless solutions to the many enigmas we contemplate today, and will restore your faith in the coming of a New Age promised land."

In addition to the "modernized text" you will join researchers Nick Redfern, Tim Beckley and Paul David Roberts as they reveal the many mystical secrets of Mount Shasta, widely regarded as a transformational vortex. Learn of inner earth entrances, the man who lives forever, the existence of Bigfoot on Mount Shasta, and ghost stories that will thrill you.

The book is fully illustrated and graphically designed by "Adman" William Kern. Printed in large format, it will captivate and entice the reader and provoke much thought.

Order The Secrets Of Mount Shasta and A Dweller On Two Planets for $22.00 + 5.00 S/H.

WANT TO LEARN MORE?
If you missed our earlier work
MYSTERIES OF MOUNT SHASTA: HOME OF THE UNDERGROUND DWELLERS AND ANCIENTS GODS simply add $20.00 to your order.
Both books will impact you greatly!
TIMOTHY G. BECKLEY, BOX 753, NEW BRUNSWICK, NJ 08903

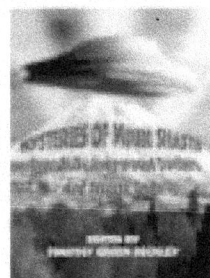

THE OUTER SPACE PEOPLE AND INNER EARTH PEOPLE

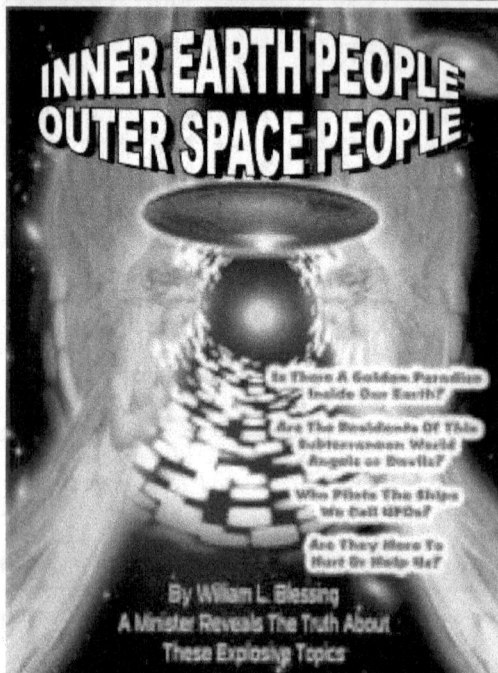

INNER EARTH PEOPLE OUTER SPACE PEOPLE

Is There A Golden Paradise Inside Our Earth?

Are The Residents Of This Subterranean World Angels or Devils?

Who Pilots The Ships We Call UFOs?

Are They Here To Hurt Or Help Me?

By William L. Blessing
A Minister Reveals The Truth About These Explosive Topics

Censored For Centuries By The Church With The Backing Of World Leaders!

Is There A Golden Paradise Inside Our Earth?

Who Pilots The Ships We Call UFOs?

Are They Here To Harm Or Help Us?

Are the Residents Of This Subterranean World Angels Or Devils?

Quietly – without public fanfare – scientists search for the entrance to the inner Earth. Such a discover could possibly improve all our lives . . .as well as provide an endless source for fossil fuel.

It could be that mankind may not be alone *on* this planet. Scripture actually speaks of a paradise inside the Earth inhabited by giant plants, mythological creatures and even highly advanced human-like beings. Furthermore, UFOs *do* exist, but only some of them come from outer space. And that ones that do come here from other planets may not be peaceful. We may have to learn to protect ourselves from their ungodly influences and desires.

The author, William L. Blessing is a full gospel minister who wants to share this vital information with you! Based on Scripture, Rev.Blessing is convinced that there are "three heavens that belong to the Earth. The Apostle Paul tells us that he was 'caught up to the third heaven' (II Cor. 12:2) and while in that heaven he 'heard unspeakable words which it is not lawful for a man to utter.' (II Cor. 12:4)." Blessing states that this area of "darkness" is inhabited by a very evil people. Beyond the darkness is the moon and then the asteroid or planetoid ring of inhabited places – inhabited by the outer space people. Beyond this first heaven is a vaporous ring in which there are great quantities of ice."

According to Blessing, "The Bible teaches us that there are people dwelling in the inside of the Earth. For want of a better name I shall call them Inner Earth People. I would estimate the population of the inner Earth to be ten billion, or about five times more than those of us who live on the surface of the earth.

"There are 200,000,000 pilots in the flying saucer corps in the inner Earth. The name of their commander-in-chief is Apollyon – 'whose name in the Hebrew tongue is Abaddon, but in the Greek tongue hath his name Apollyon (Rev 9:11).'" Blessing states : "They will soon, very soon, invade the surface of the Earth. In fact, I believe that the invasion has already begun by an advance reconnaissance force that is flying out and over the sur-

Continued on next page >

face of the Earth, mapping the land areas and strategic places where they will strike in their all-out invasion!"

DRAMATIC CONTENTS INCLUDES:
Invasions Of This Earth By Outer Space People.
Cities In The Sky.
The Treasures Of The Snow.
Invisible People In The Sea And Air.
Our Three Bodies.
The Double Senses.
Our Past, Present And Future Life.
Parapsychology.
The Sublime Message.
The Awakening.
The Great Pyramid.
Great Wonders Replenish The Earth.

INNER EARTH PEOPLE & OUTER SPACE PEOPLE is not a small, insignificant, book. It is well over 300 large formatted – 8.5x11 – pages, weighing over two pounds. It is crammed packed with never before released data on a subject that has been neglected by the media and not even whispered about by our cleric, even though Rev. Blessing says it is a specific part of the Holy Scripture. Not only does Blessing draw upon Biblical references, but also from world headlines, personal experience and the words of others not prone to elaboration.

Dr. Blessings work retails on the internet and through other sources for $29.95, but we are offering it to our loyal readers for just **$25.00 + $5.00 S/H**

Inner Light · Box 753 · New Brunswick, NJ 08903
PayPal Orders MRUFO8@hotmail.com   Phone 732 602-3407

WANT TO LEARN MORE?

Flying Saucers Come From Beneath The Earth– And Other Inner Earth Mysteries – 150 minutes – on two DVDs.

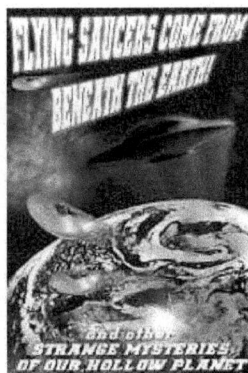

REVIEWS:

Conspiracy Journal.com
"Well edited. Guaranteed to shock and alarm those who are unfamiliar with the data on the Hollow Earth Mysteries."
Cinema Journal
"Science Fiction??? Science Reality??? Or aspiring chilling conspiracy??? You be the judge!"

PRODUCT DESCRIPTION

COVERUP? CONSPIRACY? SCIENTIFIC FACT? Or INSANE FICTION? This DVD explores what may be the greatest unexplained mystery of our planet, which both scientific and government agencies have long sought to keep under wraps for security reasons. Here is evidence ***THE EARTH IS HOLLOW AND POPULATED BY A RACE OF SUPER BEINGS!*** This 2-disc set runs nearly 4 hours and includes rare newsreel footage of Admiral Byrd's alleged trip inside of our planet. ***WEIRD ALTERNATIVE SCIENCE YOU WILL FIND NO WHERE ELSE!*** Includes presentation by James Crenshaw, editor of HollowEarthInsider.com

SPECIAL OFFER
Add $25.00 to your order to receive book and DVD set!
$50.00 total + $5.00 S/H

www.ingramcontent.com/pod-product-compliance
Lightning Source LLC
Chambersburg PA
CBHW080330270326
41927CB00014B/3165